SEMIOTEXT (E)

Subscription & Renewal Form

Please enter my subscription to **SEMIOTEXT(E)**
beginning with issue number _____

☐ New Subscription

☐ Renewal

NAME

INSTITUTION (University, Library, Research Center)

ADDRESS

CITY   STATE   ZIP

COUNTRY

Please Check One:

Subscription Rates (1 year/3 issues)

☐ Institution $24.00
☐ Regular $12.00
☐ Student $11.00

Foreign subscribers please add $3.00 for postage.

$ _____ enclosed

Semiotext(e)
FOREIGN AGENTS SERIES

Jim Fleming and Sylvere Lotringer, Series Editors

IN THE SHADOW OF THE SILENT MAJORITIES
Jean Baudrillard
$3.95

ON THE LINE
Gilles Deleuze and Felix Guattari
$3.95

DRIFTWORKS
Jean-Francois Lyotard
$3.95

R DEFENSE AND ECOLOGICAL STRUGGLES
Paul Virilio
$3.95

SIMULATIONS
Jean Baudrillard
$3.95

THE SOCIAL FACTORY
Toni Negri and Mario Tronti
$3.95

PURE WAR
Paul Virilio
$4.95

FORGET FOUCAULT
Jean Baudrillard
$3.95

METATRON: RECORDING ANGEL
Sol Yurick
$3.95

SEMIOTEXT (E), 522 Philosophy Hall, Columbia University, New York, NY 10027

Please send titles circled above. I enclose $ _____ (include $1 postage)

Semiotext(e)
FOREIGN AGENTS SERIES

Jim Fleming and Sylvere Lotringer, Series Editors

IN THE SHADOW OF THE SILENT MAJORITIES
Jean Baudrillard
$3.95

ON THE LINE
Gilles Deleuze and Felix Guattari
$3.95

DRIFTWORKS
Jean-Francois Lyotard
$3.95

POPULAR DEFENSE AND ECOLOGICAL STRUGGLES
Paul Virilio
$3.95

SIMULATIONS
Jean Baudrillard
$3.95

THE SOCIAL FACTORY
Toni Negri and Mario Tronti
$3.95

PURE WAR
Paul Virilio
$4.95

FORGET FOUCAULT
Jean Baudrillard
$3.95

METATRON: RECORDING ANGEL
Sol Yurick
$3.95

SEMIOTEXT (E), 522 Philosophy Hall, Columbia University, New York, NY 10027

Please send titles circled above. I enclose $ _____ (include $1 postage)

SEMIOTEXT (E)

Subscription & Renewal Form

Please enter my subscription to **SEMIOTEXT(E)** beginning with issue number _____

☐ New Subscription

☐ Renewal

Please Check One:

Subscription Rates (1 year/3 issues)

☐ Institution $24.00
☐ Regular $12.00
☐ Student $11.00

Foreign subscribers please add $3.00 for postage.

NAME

INSTITUTION (University, Library, Research Center)

ADDRESS

CITY   STATE   ZIP

COUNTRY

$ _____ enclosed

O A S I S

SEMIOTEXT(E)

O A S I S

Editorial Group

Timothy Simone
Peter Caravetta
Frank Mecklenburg
Brigitte Ouvry-Vial
Gregory Whitehead

Production Assistants

Martim Avillez Pam Ahern
George Alexander Arnold
Barkus Jim Fleming Peter
Gente Atina Grossman
Leandro Katz (cover
photograph) Don Quinn
Kelly Maria Nadotti Mary
Paige Heidi Paris Sam
Schoenbaum Tal Yerden

All editorial correspondence
for the issue should be addressed to OASIS 295 E. 8th
St., New York, New York
10009 USA

OASIS

SEMIOTEXT(E)

semiotext(e)

522 philosophy hall
columbia university
n.y., n.y. 10027
(212)-280-3956

volume IV, number 3, 1984
general editor: sylvere lotringer
managing editor: jim fleming
copyright by semiotext(e), inc.
ISSN 0 093 95779
subscriptions (three issues)
individuals $12.00
institutions $24.00

OASIS

O A S I S

Rock of Ages

Minus Delta t

The rock is picked up in Wales (UK) and relocated in the Himalayas. The rock is charged (in value) with the energy that is procured by *minus Delta t* to carry out the transportation. Like a sculpture, but without the chisel, it becomes a monument. This rock has never been ordered to the Himalayas, nor was its removal from England requested — except for *minus Delta t*. The rock weighs about 7 tons and was initially intended for construction purposes, Stonehenge, but never made it out of the quarry. The distance for the *Bangkok Project* is 19967 kilometers and figures as the basis for value calculation. The cost for 1 meter of ground covered is 2 German Pfennigs.

That means: 1 kilometer = 1 share = 20 German Marks = 20 Swiss Francs = 150 Austrian Shillings = 50 French Francs = 11000 Italian Lire = 5 English Pounds with due regards to exchange fluctuations.

The purchase of shares will 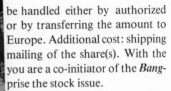 be handled either by authorized stockbrokers, or by cash payment, or by transferring the amount to one of the project accounts in Europe. Additional cost: shipping expenses (2 German Marks) for the mailing of the share(s). With the purchase of one or more shares you are a co-initiator of the *Bangkok Project*. 19967 shares comprise the stock issue.

The holder of one or more shares, after the relocation of the rock in the Himalayas has the right of codetermination concerning the destiny of the monument. The rock belongs to the European art market and thus the value of the shares may increase. After the conclusion of the *Bangkok Project*, a meeting of stockholders will be held, possibly in a sports stadium. It may be decided, for instance, that the rock remains as it is and where it is, or that it will be transported back in its entirety, or that each stockholder has the right to knock off one's share of the rock in Asia, etc.

Initially, transportation has been a technical problem; today, transportation is a bureaucratic problem. The cultural content looses its significance at the Bosphorus, i.e.that the cultural content of the rock-form shifts as continuously as the rock itself. Everybody knows: When such a transportation happens on the road it is no coincidence—it is the catalyst's effect of a rock on a tractor truck.

translation by Frank Mecklenburg

The Entertainer

Joseph Saruva

The sun has long set behind the thickly forested mountains of the Central Ranges in the Highlands of New Guinea. Smoke from many fires can be seen snaking into the sky against the dark shadowy forms of the towering mountains. Shouts echo from the care-free children playing the universal game of hide and seek. Women can be seen moving briskly about their business, carrying out normal female chores. Here and there are groups of men passing time, discussing their day's achievements or future plans.

This is the evening scene in the village of Kanakaiufa, balanced on a very narrow crest, bounded on all sides by the soaring mountains of the central cordillera. Practically unblemished by western civilization, this village had been unaware of the world beyond the mountains until fairly recent times. The only contact the people of Kanakaiufa have with the world beyond the mountains is the occasional administration patrol which comes through this village.

It was during one of these patrols that the people were told of the coming of the **Namba Wan Man.** They were also told that many people from distant places were coming together at Goroka to see and welcome the **Big Man** or the **Namba Wan Man.**

So the women moving around briskly and the men talking in groups did have some hidden significance. Suddenly, the stillness of the mountain evening air was rudely shattered by a deafening clangour. A metallic object looking like an axle from a bygone vehicle, suspended by a cane in front of a house, was savagely hammered by the Luluai's son, with the head of an axe.

The noise summoned the villagers to a gathering in front of the Luluai's house. Within seconds, the villagers hurried to his house. All the people in the village turned up for the meeting. Despite the large crowd, there was complete silence.

Presently, the eyes of everyone were fixed on the elderly figure of the Luluai, the headman of the Kanakaiufas — a man respected and admired by all both as a warrior and as a leader. Having made himself comfortable on a large stone in front of his subjects, he slowly but distinctly raised his right hand. After clearing his throat, he addressed the people. *My people, can you all remember the time we all went to a very very big sing-sing at Koroka?* referring to one of the goroka Agricultural Shows.

Nodding of heads and whispers of confirmation assured the Luluai they all remembered the occasion. They recalled the biggest gathering they had ever seen. *Well,* the Luluai resumed, *There's another gathering similar to that one at Koroka, after two moons.* He held up two fingers indicating the two months. The old man looked around and then continued. *There's going to be a very big sing-sing to make the Nama Wan Man happy. He is Ingilis.* Murmurs and whispers of surprise and astonishment, oos and ees arose from the crowd. *Namba Wan Man,* and *Ingilis* — a term

15

used to refer to any white person — were whispered by everyone. *I have made up my mind,* continued the old man, *that we must take part in the sing-sing and we have only two moons to get ready.* Having said this, the old man raised both his hands indicating that he had finished what he had wanted to tell them.

The old man waited for any queries, but, receiving none, told the villagers that they could go back to their houses. The chief's decision was final. The idea of making the **Namba Wan Man** happy was relished by everyone. The people would prepare for the day — putting together of head dresses, fixing up of bows and arrows and the making of masks.

The weeks that followed saw the villagers labouring in earnest — preparing for the big day. Two weeks was allowed for the journey. When all was ready, the older people and some of the people who were not in the Goroka trip came and grabbed and hugged those who were going. The long talks which were uttered during this scene were no doubt good wishes for a safe journey and return.

The journey from Kanakaiufa was a long, tiring business. The progress during the first three days was good, covering about fifteen to twenty miles a day. After this, progress was rather slow, as the people, especially the women and children, began to show exhaustion. Typical cold rain of the highlands poured down on the fifth day of the journey.

Although the men had quickly put up crude huts to protect them from the rain, everyone was cold and miserable. On the sixth day, the rain stopped and as the sun slowly broke through the clouds, the people resumed their journey, but progress was still slow. On the seventh day a sorry looking group of people arrived at Minj.

However, here the people found that there were none of those big noisy things which ran on round legs waiting for them. The people decided to spend the night at Minj. Early next morning the people got up and started the long journey towards Goroka. Occasionally, the daring ones attempted to hitch-hike, but in all cases they were made to spring back to the ditch as the big things gathered speed down the road.

After a day's journey from Minj down the great Highlands Highway, the Kanakaiufas camped for the night. They found that there were many people on the road and the general course of the journey showed that, like them, they were heading for Goroka. They were all included in this one big game of fun of making the **Namba Wan Man** happy. Hating to walk during the hot part of the day, the people left very early next morning and by midday they had travelled about ten or twelve miles. Having been on the move for just over a week, progress during the day was slow but the people made up for it during their early morning walks. It was sheer determination that kept them moving all the time.

Just when all hope of getting to Goroka in time seemed lost, one of those big noisy monsters was heard coming from Hagen way. So deafening and terrifying was the noise that some of the people took to the bush. It seemed as if it was a god-sent monster, because the driver, who was from Minj, stopped when he saw the people. The driver made signs for the people to go on the truck. Those who took shelter in the bush were called back.

With the help of the driver, the bilums containing kaukaus and bundles — no doubt containing the valuable feathers — were hustled onto the truck. There was fear and excitement as the truck started off. Everytime another truck passed, the people lay flat on top of each other with fright.

So happy were the people that they never stopped singing all the way to Goroka. It was late in the afternoon when they arrived there. As the truck moved off the people discussed where they were going to sleep. There was one man who was doing most of the talking — it was Hati. Holding tightly on to one of his hands was Natini, his son, who had survived the trip. Hati told the people that they should go to where they had stayed last time they came here. At this moment, two figures approached the group. They were some Luluais of this place, as they had shiny small things made of metal stuck on their shirts. After an exchange of words, the two men led the people away. They were shown some crude huts where they could stay. As everyone settled down for the night, the old man from Kanakaiufa told his people to be up early and get ready to welcome the **Namba Wan Man.**

It was not yet daylight, but the people were up already. The little camp was full of life — men, women and children moving around very briskly. Over their heads were multi-coloured feathers forming the head-dress. Near the forehead of each person was a set of neatly attached plumes of the bird of paradise. Faces were concealed with colourfully decorated masks. Those men without masks together with the women wore king shells around their necks, and long thin bones and feathers through their noses. The faces were painted with mud and charcoal. Whatever was put on was done with great care. Nothing was to go wrong. They had not forgotten that they were to make the **Namba Wan Man** happy. They were not to dissappoint him. The old man of the Kanakaiufas strolled around looking at all. He was proud of his little group. He nodded his head in approval.

The bright rays of the morning sun promised good weather. All this time no one had given any thought for food, except one person. A woman was talking to a small boy, probably advising him. Yes, she was telling him what to do. As she gave him a baked kaukau, she said: *Stay close to me, Natini, and don't leave me whatever you do.* This was Woku advising her son. Natini, quietly gnawing the kaukau, nodded his head in confirmation. Just then, a figure covered with a enormous head-dress approached the mother and her son. It was Hati, looking his best and holding a set of arrows and a bow.

At this moment, the singing of hundreds of people dancing as they came along the road held everyone's gaze. The big head-dresses swayed with the rhythmic movements of the dancers. This was the signal for everyone to join in the big welcome sing-sing. Then the Luluai of the Kanakaiufas told everyone to get ready to move. They all joined the singing group. Traffic was stopped, as the road was full of dancing people. The dancers proceeded towards the airstrip. They were all led and directed by people who were blue clothes. Natini was having trouble understanding all that he saw. The people who had different color skins, wearing strange clothes, baffled him. He tried to sort out just why people who had the same color skin as himself wore similar clothes to those people with white skins.

There were many other things which were equally amazing and which his little mind refused to make any sense of. Within his heart he thanked his kind parents for letting him come with them. Suddenly a jerk on his hand by his mother brought him back from his dream world. There was a renewed vigour and excitement in the dancers. The **Big Man** had arrived. The people danced and sang like they had never done before. What a spectacular sight! The people whom time had forgotten had been somehow brought together for a common aim — to please the **Namba Wan Man.** The feeling of tribalism was momentarily forgotten. Everyone's attention was focused on a group of people standing on a platform. Everyone pushed and shoved in an effort to see better. As for some, they could hardly see a thing because of the throng in front. Among the disappointed were Natini and Woku.

I can't see mother, said Natini, almost in tears.

I can't see either, replied Woku, rather disappointed. Then close by, someone said: *Which is the Namba Wan Man?*

That one there with blue clothes and holding a thing like a knife, was the reply.

But there are two of them dressed the same, someone put in. *Which one is it? Must be the tall one standing in the middle.* The guessers continued in frustration. Natini and his mother had given up searching for a place to see better. Then Hati, after looking around for his family for quite some time, came and stood by them. *We can't see the man,* said Woku with a tone of disappointment in her voice. *Lift me up, father. I want to see this Namba Wan Man,* pleaded Natini. Handing the bow and arrows to his wife, Hati hoisted Natini upon his shoulders. *It's useless father, I can't see a thing. The head-dresses are stopping the view.* Then someone who was up in a tree shouted that the group of people was getting into a small thing on round legs. *It's moving away,* was the tree person's cry. Utter disappointment showed markedly on the faces of Hati, Woku and Natini. The mass of people started moving away, still dancing and singing. Hati, Woku and Natini were rather quiet and gloomy. Woku with hatred in her voice, said: *I can't understand why the people still want to sing and dance.*

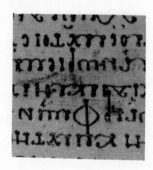

Big Fish

Leslie Dick

Passive action: she moved because she had to, his job. Neither in pursuit, nor fugitive, she merely repeated. She can tell you almost nothing about the geography or history or politics of the countries she lived in: that was his department. Her task was to reconstruct, over and over, the american house, the american children, the american cocktail party — under adverse conditions. London 1967, Ankara 1959, The Hague 1953, her social circle consisted of the other americans, like them. She describes the satisfactions of expatriatism as being a big fish in a small puddle (*In Turkey there aren't five thousand of you, people like you, there are maybe 300.*) Being seen to be glamourous and interesting by their acquaintance in New York, she enjoyed being praised, admired for her daring, her ability to prevail — even in a clapboard house in Casper Wyoming, smelling of the oil refinery, stained with red dust. She imagined that her children would become *interna*tional: They would speak about five languages, they wouldn't be thrown if things were done in a different manner, they wouldn't freak out at a foreign word on a menu. She became very good at cobbling together expressions out of her smattering of french and italian, and excelled in the enthusiastic mime that makes requests. Her husband spoke no languages (the language of the oil company), he watched her willingness to appear foolish with embarrassment, gratitude. The children turned out to speak no foreign languages whatsoever. While she takes no responsibility for these changes, these twenty five houses she has lived in, twenty nine moves she had made, she did once refuse to go live in Saskatchewan, in 1956, evidence of some power to choose.

The site of the move itself is not the country, the landscape, architecture, or her state of mind, but the innumerable objects, possessions, *belongings* that come and go, that move. Her emotional priority is to sustain a continuity of things in the discontinuity of place. The same furniture, the same layout, — the same bed, a bedroom repeated, — no difference, for difference in this movement, signifies loss. To move a whole house is to handle, to possess, pack, store, discard, keep. Her moving practice reaffirms her (self) possession. It is a chance to clear out: *It's a relief, you always get rid of some of the less important things.* Her classic, epic move was to Turkey, for two years, in 1958; she was given the list by the corporation, and shopped for six months to accumulate the necessary gear. *We just bought everything, from safety pins to bandaids to hairspray to shoelaces, — two years supply of powdered milk, worcestershire sauce for bloody marys...* a stove, refrigerator, television, piano, — when she told a friend who had lived there that she was taking a toilet seat, he said take a toilet. She did, and beds, furniture, kleenex, clothes for the children to grow into, a nanny, two girl children under five, trailing dolls, dolls clothes, paper dolls, crayons, coloring books, endlessly. She took christmas presents, thinking ahead. All this stuff installed in a white sub-international style apartment block (post-war, unfinished) on a brown scrubby hill outside Ankara, surrounded by muddy, dusty fields, and abject poverty, large families living in mud huts, doing without, underprivileged. While the americans in the concrete tower lived out nuclear family life, — as if, removed from its context, displaced, the system of the american family becomes elementary, standing out in grotesque kodachrome, mommy daddy and the kids, outlined against the dusty background, the family snap.

Her parents have lived in the same house for 46 years, and it is this house she names, un-thinking, home. In a sense, the american house she reconstitutes in different places is an approx-imation of that paternal house: comfy, old-fashioned furniture, with an elegant aspect, a class display. In her houses, dissatisfaction, the unhappy compromise, is built in. No place is quite right, no shift without disappointment: partly because the shift is what is felt, dismantling, reconstruct-ing. It is the transaction that resonates, while the place itself, difference, is only recognised when the decision comes once again to move. She is inattentive to anything that cannot be included in her practice of repetition, recovery, restoration — the view from the window is insignificant, she is in-different, and discontented, for unhappily one cannot move and still have everything. When she is forced to leave a place, momentarily she mourns it, sees it as if for the first time, as lost. That is as close as she comes.

Mosque Sauvage

Mustafa Isrui

During the war of Beirut in the summer of 1982, Col. Muammar Qadaffi announced, ad-midst indications that the PLO would indeed evacuate the city, that the PLO should remain and commit suicide in the face of an apparent Israeli victory. Despite Qadaffi's Homra-bred nostalgia for literality, something more than a sacrifice of the body was being suggested. The colonel was instructing the troops to disappear; to go into the capitals of the world, learn their ways and forget about them; to blend into the multitudes, the array of colors that have begun to fill even the whitest places. Where once the Palestinian cause was seen as the vehicle to unmoor Arabs from traditions of internecine rivalry and as the means to redefine the Arab world, Qadaffi understood that the Palestinian movement, as a military machine, had become caught in the old conflicts among Arab shieks increasingly dependent upon the Israeli threat as the means through which to sustain their power. The army which was to cohere the tongues of Mecca now becomes scattered through-out the fiefdoms, condemned to endless pool games in decaying resort cities. Qadaffi's implication is that the Third World must dis-appear, cease to exist as some-thing it never was — an identifi-able force mistaking its modalities of resistance for its images of nationhood.

The war against the West cannot be won; the reduction of traditional cultures into appen-dices of Western portfolios can-not be refused. Every large-scale attempt to articulate a refusal usually becomes a despotic guarantor of that refusal. Yet every attempt to modernize and dissociate from tradition inevitably means becoming normalized to Western standards; there is no modernization in alternative terms. Every attempt to juggle submission to Western normalization with a resistance to its domination provokes anxieties and questions about the authenticity and integrity of the juggler. The psychological terms in which dependency on the West is considered are themselves Western constructions enveloping the Third World questioner into a dependency on the West's romance with insufficiency.

Cafes in Third World capitals become immersed in a drone of proliferating and irresolvable inquiries: What was the basis of our attraction to the West? When a person is raped what kind of a mind does he have to mirror himself after the rapist or victim? Why did we start laying down with their women; why did we want their refrigerators, their fancy watches and cinematic techniques? What deals did our fathers and mothers make with them to gain advantage over our grandparents?

In the prime ministeries there is much talk of a North-South dialogue, of a new world order. Just as socialism is usually used to conceal the revitalized nationalistic tendencies of despots, the Third World has no assurance that the idealistic ruminations of a coordinated and coherent world are not the means through which the West will articulate and implement a revised form of domination.

The encroachment of the modern operated through providing villagers and tribesmen with the possibility of a flight and exit previously unknown to them. Suddenly there existed some outside world which compelled them to evaluate and scrutinize social positions previously left unexamined. The crux of the imperial barrage of an exterior was the supplementing of a traditional circuit of population movement and individual journeying with the possibility of a space completely unencumbered by the requirement to return, actually or symbolically, to the site of one's origins. There have always been those villagers who have left and disappeared, who have engaged in what the Hausa called Ywon Dandi, the walk of the world. During times of social stress, villagers, individually and collectively, have migrated. But the migration has been motivated by the need to stretch the village walls, to elaborate an inside and to extend the village beyond the capacity to make sense of its strictures. Those that left the village merely shifted and relocated its borders, not to make the village disappear, but to diversify and enrich it.

Upon the outset of modernization, the basis of this movement was altered. Modernity became an exit to be bought, not only for oneself but for the clan one hopes to displace as the primary anchorage of one's economic and moral existence. The village could be made to disappear. For the migrant to emerge from the strictures of the clan he must first uproot the entirety of his kin from its village. And the village must dissociate itself entirely from its tribal and regional bodies. This methodology of movement is why the efforts of progressive Third World states to de-link from the West often embody the same strategic maneuvers used by these states to originally affiliate with the West.

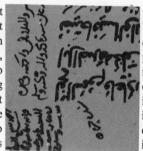

Third World fighters must now seize upon the lingering difference that continues to exist between them and the West. In the West people say little to each other but know everything about each other; in the Third World, people say much but know little Our strength was our capacity to mingle with each other without having to know what was going on as the precondition. We in the Third World know exactly what is happening to us, and the knowledge itself burdens us with the incessant questioning of our capacities. Seduced by the West into defending ourselves, we turn the West into the judge and ourselves into co-conspirators, futilely hoping, in this symbiosis, for an energizing of our indigenous power.

The position for the Third World fighter to assume is one of overt defeat, draining himself of aspirations and traces of a desire for upward mobility; to act as if the substance of one's life is gone and the emptiness of tomorrow a foregone conclusion. Just as thousands of Bidan and Haradin refugees line up in Russo and Nouakchott each morning for the UN allotment of grain, just as Tuareg and Fulani drought victims sleep the day away in the muddy troughs made by government cement trucks in Katsinda and Zinder, we must become totally dependent upon the dominator for *everything,* actively participate in the garbaging process and return to the West the absolute responsibility for whether we live or die. For there can be no vindicating nationhood, no liberated zone free of the process by which we are simultaneously converted into the impediments of progress and the conscience of Western narcissism.

The power of the West resides in its ability to entice the Third World into attempts to seize power as if that which the Third World finds impossible can be altered. In the process, through this diabolically engineered defeat of the Third World, the West garners strength and legitimacy. The West must create its own threat so as to defeat that which threatens, which can never threaten since the means for exerting that threat operate through channels the West itself constructs.

Qadaffi, the lucky hyena that rails against the empire from behind a bank of TV cameras in his desert tent, understands that each beast requires the irrational melee and the barroom brawl.

His madness is that he already acts the defeated man, the man who will provoke wars he cannot possibly win because he is indifferent to the outcome, who knows that the only way for the Third World to survive is to mingle among the displaced populations knowing nothing and remembering nothing except the time of day handouts are provided.

For our land is not even their land anymore. Who will we seize it from? Who will they turn to if we go away and cease to be ourselves, mix with the thousands of westerners initiated into permanent states of unemployment. Carrying our mosques on our backs we go away from the white man's conspiracy of symbols and his preoccupation with elaborating and confounding a fate so treacherously simple and elegant. Away from his need to make everything uncertain, his need for us to threaten him, to howl like the dogs he is predestined to find at the back door, unhinged.

والحسن بكر منصور تعالى دفنتا بها مو نكرما حمد
المهند عزيزا ابن ابو سعيد تمكنه فا الشيخ الاعلم
ابنل ابو القسم عثمان ... طام اعلا فك بها ... الغر
... ابو الحسن ... الجوار ... الظاهر
الله ... الشافعي وسترة السر ابو القسم ... حمد
ريا س لا دمن شبئنا الص ... سمع الامام ... والبر
... الحجا د الثالث واولد مركبا المنشط ... ا
... عده وبعضها الفقها ... سمو كطو
... ابراحم ها يوم السبت السابع و
... الشعر به ... لبقته وصلواتة على حمد

Sand in the Mouth

Franco Beraldi

(Bifo)

Whenever a social universe forms adequate to the technological and communications potential of actual social brainpower, we call it Renaissance. A Renaissance implies the establishment of an entirely new perspective on both social world and political territory. That's why every Renaissance implies a crossing of the desert. Little by little, the desert reveals unforeseen scenery, scenery that could never have been predicted within the coordinates and survey apparatus inherited from the old world, the sightings eluding the *pre*dominant apparatus. When you acknowledge the desert in the Metropolis, your nomadic journey begins. Until you learn to see again, from here on the desert will never end. What is to be changed is no longer the *world,* but our *in*sight, the rules according to which we construct and enter the territory around us. Let us look at the present not as a time of crisis for a partic-ular social model but rather as a time of overlay, overlay of in-sightings, of two universes, two models of how it is we get the lay of the land. And let us not insist on thinking of such an overlay as a dialectical overtaking, but think instead of schismogenesis, auto-nomisation, secession.

The center of my reflec-tion is as follows: the conditions of change for the statutes of know-ledge and for social organisation are strictly and mutually implied; they both refer to a constituting level on the anthropologic and techno-communicative planes. The condition of nomadism is rooted in the proliferation and overlay of competing models of knowledge, communication and interaction. For example, the mechanico-industrial universe founded its communication statutes upon a technology of writing. A linear, sequentially oriented technology, writing as technology modifies its object to fulfill the dreams of its own order. The fully accomplished historical product of writing is *industry,* the production of an Umwelt based on principles of sequence, machinic repetitiousness and a discrete transmission of signals. Writing does not simply reduplicate the spoken word. Verba volant scripta manet. Writing *takes over* whole territories of thought, establishes the conditions for *logical* reasoning and links together experience into a relentless chain of signifiers. In this way, writing colonizes insight and knowledge and rules the imaginary according to a strict and obsessive principle of identity.

The electronisation of communications technologies and the informatisation of social networks introduce a mutation into the universe that had been mapped out through the technology of writing. With the proliferation of signs and the mushrooming of transmissions, both possible and realized, the world as seen, as sighted, as surveyed from the old mechanical perspective is no longer comprehensible. We now find a world transformed into an infosphere where every object is a carrier of information, a strange tracing of a pre-literate, animistic world; wherever the telecommunications network is most thickly congealed, we find that attention to magic flourishes. The deep anthropologic strata that the industrial city had tried to bury, homologate, integrate, rise to the surface amidst a rapid dissolve of urban and industrial territoriality.

With this mutating overlay, the diffusion of electronic communications technologies complicates the familiar dynamics of capital colonisation. On one side, electronics give capital colonisation a tremendous opening, possibilities of speed and depth of penetration that no mechanical technology has ever been able to display. But at the same time, electronics also fosters a principle of decay; the hierarchical ordering and bi- univocal correspondence between sender and receiver come under question. So does the possibility of accurately quantifying and measuring human activity, most importantly, labor power. The social necessity of factory work, work that can be tabulated, is over; the law of value is kaput. Further, the necessity of territorial permanence deteriorates at a rapidly accelerating pace. Social molecules no longer take *place.* Consequently, the urban shape becomes unrecognizable, empty, deserted. In a way that has no precedent in human history, militarization becomes the model, the only available model, for every form of social interaction as well as the imaginary. *From overlay, mutation and from mutation, war.*

The new infosphere works with deterritorialization, movement, circulation. The informatisation of the production process and of the circulation of goods itself (information is, after all, a good par excellence), makes any reference to territory more and more evanescent, vague, useless. The reality of social domination is no longer linked to materialized territory. The actual territory upon which power grounds itself is invisible, or at least without place. In the dimension of everyday life, in the no-place utopia of concrete communication, there is only the desert. Inside the desert, the telecommunications system creates the conditions for a new kind of nomadism; social life becomes tribal. We pass from a system of communication that is unitarian and centralized, undifferentiated and universal, imposing the same message on everyone, to the possibility of communications networks ever more diversified and dispersed. Differences among the videoelectronic tribes become ever more untranslateable; and the chance of non-identification is the chance of escape, or at least oasis. Renaissance presupposes secession, and secession involves a process of cutting loose, already prefigured in the camps and caravans of the vast contemporary desert. Nomadic mobility permits an exit from the most devastating consequences of the crisis, finding residual conditions for residual life. Surely this nomadic population is the best equipped to survive the possible futures of planetary catastrophe, war, famine. So let us move, together, away from the no-place utopia, *and into the desert!*

translation by Paula Casanova

26

The Invention of Life

Theo Kneubuehler

Prelude The question of position. Where are you? Are you anyplace at all? (Who is that *you*? Martin Disler, me, an idea, a possibility, an ideal, a question?) You are not above, beneath, behind, in front. You are right in the middle and the middle is wherever there is an inside of something. Is inside a position? Can you *take* this position? No, you are in there, and being there means being on the move, movement from one center to another. What's in between? The being on your way. And what and where is that way, since you can't just simply be on the move? That way is stumbling, flying, questioning, looking, sensing, feeling. It might be a spiral, dead ahead, it might be a circle, it might be liana loops in jungle trees, it might be furrows across the fields. I can already hear those who say: *How do you keep your distance?* The answer: *The distance results from the degree of expenditure.*

Expenditure means that while acting, you turn to the center, let the center grow from inside out. The center is not the projection of something that happened before, but a sudden arrival after active preparations. The degree of fragility is high. In other words, you don't want to be as placed as so many others. *You* want to use your energies differently. *Your* task is the task of the mutant.

You want to be vessel and stream. At the same time, the tool you produced the vessel with might alter it. Sometimes the tool, then again the vessel, some-times even the stream. Then one body is altogether and at the same time the vessel, the stream and the tool, therefore a *different* body, a mutated body, much more complicated than anything you'll ever find in the anatomy books. The potentiality of such a body is great.

Nevertheless, the versatility of these multiple activities makes you very vulnerable. Since you can't possess anything; you can't possess anything because possession is the tool minus stream and vessel, or the filled vessel without stream nor tool. Possession is a facet, a chance fragment, an amputation.

What has been written up until now is an image (which explains who or what that *you* is). The image is not the substance from which it is made; the image is its antecedents and its aftermath. In other words: the image never heads for where it's coming from. Text clear — I am not an image, you are not an image, he is not an image. The place of the image is in the living body, the living body that is inseparable from thought.

Most people sleep very deeply. Some are waking up, others already awoke, very few were awake to begin with. I want to mention a newly found fragment from Intrasophus: *Where there is a dream, no sleeper has to be.* Later, of course, the same Intrasophus tells us: *Where there is a dream, no sleeper shall be.* One word about the text. I imagine a text of radical disbelief, pure, crystalline, a text without solution, full of evasion *taken to the third degree.*

27

The First Body   The body on the way thither runs alongside walls, through the underpass, over staircases, walks through this door and leaves through that door. The body goes hither, thither, it sweats, opens the pores, the skin breathes. The body is on its way, it escapes itself to gain force within the emerging span. Loiter, delay, haste, wait, hop, postpone, dance, withhold. The tension grows, energies accumulate. Driving on highways, in narrow alleys, jams, waiting and moving, the body vessel fills up. Tense nerves, powerful heart beat, pain. The tension reaches its peak, strain, discharge, expenditure. The body spent.

The Second Body   Activity develops in the space between bodies. The second body (the image) arises from the overflow of the first body as the result of its expenditure. Response is not a echo, but a challenge. The situation is determined by communication, through feedback. As in any form of communication, the mastering of emotions plays a certain role. The second body is not simply created by desire or denial, not simply by attraction or repulsion, but by the complex penetration of movements, in reaction to what the other wants to push away, the quick change of frictions. When a gesture of the second body responds with flimsiness then the first body responds by overflooding. Then the second body gives resinous transparency, so from the friction a third form results. To the extent of gaining anybody out there, where the image spreads and lets itself develop, the first body empties out: loss of potential through expenditure. One vessel leaks, the other fills up. Between these processes, a transformation takes place. Nothing going from here to there stays the same. According to the conversation between the bodies, an image emerges which is finished when the intense strangeness *out there* indicates that a new body has resulted, detached from what the first body *knows:* asymetric duplication.

translation by Frank Mecklenburg

28

Black Sunlight

Dambudzo Marechera

Nicola sat in front of the fire peering unflinchingly into its hottest core. Tears streaked down her cheeks. Marie had taken down the old ukelele. She was singing. Susan took one look at Nicola and shouted at Marie to *STOP. STOP IT.* And kissed hugged caressed Nicola who throughout sat there confronting the redhot embers for a flame of reality. Eyes stinging, Susan slapped Nicola hard. Once. Twice. Three times. But still the girl sat there, crying silently into the fire. The wide open eye had a lurid brillance. Cold and unwinking.

Wrung out dry, those tears and fears. This grown-up silence that savaged the house with its experiments. This forever tension out there with its jackboots, gas, bullets, phlegmatic pogroms. Screwing the brains tightly into Nicola. Claiming the shit from Susan. That endless winding sheet. That penniless barefoot distance, well laid-out thorns. Lives sput-that cold unwinking hour. And Nicola's nerves, through Susan's Chris's spat-out shit. I had seen nating venom and leaping astride Chronicled it down on cold un-distilled into the last ugly droplet ing gas canisters. Smashed aside the sky askew. Letting loose a 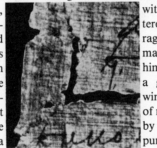 without shelter, glittering with tered, backfired. Broke down. In raged with a bitter point through maniacal intelligence, through him, Chris, simultaneously deto-a gas canister in the Square. winking film. Nauseated, fucked, of reality. Leaping astride explod-by vigilant truncheon. **Reeling,** all punch that smacked the pig's face into the back of the skull, **Staggering.** Dizzily wrenching a perspective from the teeming turmoil. **Roaring.** Screeching farts. And with stout stick crunching out of the melee. Bashing skulls left and right. A bullet nicking the button from his shirt. Run, **Running.** Side streets run, in optical trick of flying elbows and knees. Leaving no more than bloodstains and a red pillar of cloud. Made Susan mad, such useless demonstration. Sitting there, eyes glued on the TV screen where the acrimonious face of law and order was hissing mindless threats against Communists and their mindless sympathizers.

That's us Nicola said, suddenly.

Startling Susan and I.

She had smashed her way out of the glittering glass shell. Her lips curled uncertainly. Her long drab skirts now shifting as she stretched out her legs. Dabbed at her wet cheeks with rims of Kleenex. Smiling faintly. After her attack. I looked quickly at Marie. But she sat impassively. Her whole demeanour eloquently demure. Making me suddenly aware that she had always known all about it. Those brute and subversive noises. The whole thin stick on which the Black Sunlight Organization precariously sat. A thin and dry branch of a thick and tall tree that had been dead for ninety years. And as we sat in my house watching the news and thinking thoughts and campaigning against the intellect, I knew she knew one day that thin dry branch would crack and send us flying down onto the hard bloodstained ground. Fucked. Boiling with a seething martyrdom. Having smashed the boot through the glass veneer of the state. Of our nerves. And minds. That sheer blatant austerity. Is wealth. In our wake, smashed institutions. Smashed minds. Smashed traffic signs. Smashed courtrooms. Smashed armouries. Eyeballs whirring. Their red veins sticking out to encapsulate the black sunlight up there deep down here. Right here in our heritage. Leaving nothing but Bull Shit Organs.

Precariously doomed, perpetually primed. And, in that, somewhat erased, leaving only the faint outlines of caricatures. Strange and cutting. Yielding only to the preposterous inevitable end. Which would not end all. The bestial fact would always be there. To appall. To astound. To ignite into action such estranged hearts as these. For whom there could be no ending. No cutting coronary of fear to shriek one into the blind end of settling down to work and spawn. Against that dead end one cultivated something more than a mere and total impassivity. A fearful rage, blinding. An extreme revulsion, convulsing. But under a firm control. Disciplined and maniacal control of nerves. And action.

No Nicola, that's not us, Susan said impatiently.

She was right. For we did not and had never claimed responsibility for the bombings and the **happenings.** No Black Sunlight Organization existed — publicly and even privately to the Special Branch and the security forces. There were only the endless fragmented leftwing parties from which now and then we had won members. Nick. Nicola. Susan. And to stretch a point, myself. Even the very name, BSO was a joke. Bakunin Shits Okay. Bleeding Sods (cf. Orifices). Black Souls Organize. To atrophy ourselves with a BSO label was shit. I had in a moment of drunken empathy with Chris coined the thing about black sunlight and of course he had seen the other side of that blinding light. Not that he did not know whatever other side there was, he said. Hiccupped. I was trying to get him to explain how he had spiked me out of my head and with what kind of dope on my first three days at Devil's End. Fingering his necklace of bones and scratching underneath his denim shirt he had said: *Just something I picked up from a psychiatrist.*

I had demanded that he elaborate.

Well, it wasn't hypnosis, though of course there is a blind side to that, he had replied.

And passed the wineskin.

I drank, watching him. He had come through a long way. Even now — watching Susan and Nicola watching the TV news — I wondered: Had he really truly come through? There were so many false stopping and watering places. Had we all come through? I was sure of Katherine. I was sure of Susan. But that was all. I was not sure of myself. The brute and unflinching hatred was not there. But did I really register in my innermost being nothing of all this that was happening? It was impossible. I could feel the inexorable rot gradually settling in the marrow of my bones. A dark pencil-thin rim around the abyss was the dream's edge. It reached out memory's swift caress, pulsing with a cutting perception.

Nick had once written: *The goldspeaking river/Toward the wet dark/Floods the century/And my heart into the void/The lingering optimism pours.* Was it like that? Seeing through brainblood this journey's trajectory. Dreams bayonet-ripped. And every sudden glance meets in midflight the worm's sneer. It was not like that. Even for Nick when we talked endlessly into the night. Talked of what marrowed him with mortality. The pitiful roads that endlessly track a man's unseen destinations. (That time spent in the playground before the fatal knell.) That probability which curtains the Future's glass. How what I am, and will be, death created long ago. The knuckles of those conversations bruised my vision. Burst out of me, fighting, streets fallen. He did not know the fire and the hurt. He could not go with the lyre and the net. He could touch the lips and mirth. But saw everywhere evidence of mastodons. **Mastodons.** Fresh from the original mud.

Sunless

Chris Marker

This morning I was on the dock at Pidjiguiti, where everything began in 1959, when the first victims of the struggle were killed. It may be as difficult to recognize Africa in this leaden fog as it is to recognize struggle in the rather dull activity of tropical longshoremen. Rumor has it that every third-world leader coined the same phrase the morning after independence: *Now the real problems start.* Cabral never got a chance to say it, he was assassinated first. But the problems started, and went on, and are still going on. Rather unexciting problems for revolutionary romanticism: to work, to produce, to distribute, to overcome postwar exhaustion, temptations of power and privilege... History only tastes bitter to those who expected it to be sugar-coated.

My personal problem was more specific: how to film the ladies of Bissau? Apparently, the magical function of the eye was working against me there. It was in the market places of Bissau and Cape Verde that I could stare at them again with equality... I see her — she saw me — she knows that I see her — she drops me her glance, but just at an angle where it is still possible to act as though it was not addressed to me—and at the end of the real glance, straight forward, that lasted a twenty-fourth of a second, the length of a film frame.

All women have a built-in grain of indestructability, and men's task has always been to make them realize it as late as possible. African men are just as good at this task as others, but after a close look at African women, I wouldn't necessarily bet on the men.

He told me the story of the dog Hachiko: A dog waited every day for his master at the station. The master died, the dog didn't know it, and he continued to wait, all his life. People were moved and brought him food. After his death, a statue was erected in his honor, in front of which suchis and rice cakes are still placed so that the faithful soul of Hachiko will never go hungry.

Tokyo is full of these tiny legends and of mediating animals. The Mitsukoshi lion stands guard on the frontiers of what was once the empire of Mr. Okada, a great collector of french paintings, the man who hired the chateau of Versailles to celebrate the hundredth anniversary of his department stores. In the computer section, I've seen young Japanese exercising their brain muscles like the young Athenians at the palestra. They have a war to win (the History books of the future will perhaps place the battle of integrated circuits at the same level as Salamis or Agincourt) but are willing to honor the unfortunate adversary by leaving other fields to him: men's fashions this season are placed under the sign of John Kennedy.

Like an old votive turtle stationed in the corner of a field, everyday he saw Mr. Akao, the president of the Japanese Patriotic Party, trumpeting from the heights of his rolling balcony against the international communist plot. He wrote me: The automobiles of the extreme right with their flags and megaphones are part of Tokyo's landscape, Mr. Akao is their focal point. I think he'll have his statue, like the dog Hachiko, at this crossroads from which he departs only to go

33

on the battlefields. He was at Narita in the sixties: peasants fighting against the building of an airport on their land, and Mr. Akao denouncing the hand of Moscow behind everything that moved...Yurakucho is the political space of Tokyo. Once upon a time I saw a bonze pray for peace in Viet Nam there. Today, young right wing activists protest against the annexation of the Northern Islands by the Russians. Sometimes they're answered that the commercial relations of Japan with the abominable occupier of the north are a thousand times better than with the American ally who's always whining about economic aggression.

On the other sidewalk, the left has the floor. The Korean Catholic opposition leader Kim Dae Jung, kidnapped in Tokyo in '73 by the South Korean Gestapo, is threatened with a death sentence. A group has begun a hunger strike, some very young militants are trying to gather signatures in his support.

I went back to Narita for the birthday of one of the victims of the struggle. The demo was unreal, I had the impression of acting in *Brigadoon,* of waking up ten years later in the midst of the same players, with the same blue lobsters of Police, the same helmeted adolescents, the same banners, the same slogan: DOWN WITH THE AIRPORT! Only one thing has been added: the airport, precisely. But with its single runway and the barbed wire that chokes it, it looks more besieged than victorious.

My pal Hayao Yamaneko has found a solution: if the images of the present don't change, then change the images of the past. He showed me the clashes of the Sixties treated by his synthesizer. Pictures that are less deceptive, he says with the conviction of a fanatic, than those you see on television. At least they proclaim themselves to be what they are: images — not the portable and compact form of an already inaccessible reality.

Hayao calls his machine's world: the Zone — a hommage to Tarkovsky.

What Narita brought back to me, like a shattered hologram, was an intact fragment of the generation of the Sixties. If to love without illusions is still to love, I can say that I loved it. It was a generation that often exasperated me, for I didn't share its Utopia of uniting in a common struggle those who revolt against poverty and those who revolt against wealth, but it screamed out that gut reaction that better adjusted voices no longer knew how, or no longer dared to utter...I met peasants there, who had come to know themselves through the struggle. Concretely, it has failed. At the same time, all they had won in their understanding of the world could have been won only through the struggle.

As for the students, some massacred each other in the mountains in the name of revolutionary purity, while others had studied capitalism so thoroughly to fight it, that they now provide it with its best executives. Like everywhere else, the Movement had its posturers and its careerists —including, and there are some, those who made a career of martyrdom—but it carried with it all those who said, like Che Guevara that *they trembled with indignation every time an injustice is committed in the world.* They wanted to give a political meaning to their generosity, and their generosity has outlasted their politics. That's why I will never allow it to be said that youth is wasted on the young.

The youth who get together every weekend at Shinjuku obviously know that they are not on a launching pad toward real life, that they *are* life, to be eaten on the spot, like fresh donuts. It's a very simple secret, the old try to hide it, and not all the young know it. The ten year old girl who threw her friend from the 13th floor of a building after having tied her hands, because she had spoken badly of their class team, hadn't discovered it yet. Parents who demand an increase in the number of special telephone lines devoted to the prevention of children's suicides find out a little late they they had kept it all too well. Rock is an international language for spreading the secret. Another is peculiar to Tokyo...

For the Takenoko, twenty is the age of retirement. They are baby Martians, I go see them dance every Sunday in the park at Yoygi. They want people to look at them, but they don't seem to notice that people do. They live in a parallel time sphere, a kind of invisible aquarium wall separates them from the crowd they attract, and I can spend a whole afternoon contemplating the little Takenoko girl who is learning, no doubt for the first time, the customs of her planet. Beyond that, they wear dog tags, they obey a whistle, the Mafia rackets them, and with the exception of a single group made up of girls, it's always a boy who commands.

One day he writes to me: Description of a dream...More and more, my dreams find their setting in the department stores of Tokyo, the subterranean tunnels than extend them and run parallel to the city. A face appears, disappears, a trace is found, is lost, all the folklore of dreams is so much in its place that the next day, when I'm awake, I realize that I continue to seek in the basement labyrinth the presence concealed the night before. I begin to wonder if those dreams are really mine, or if they are part of a totality, of a gigantic collective dream of which the entire city may be the projection. It might suffice to pick up any one of the telephones that are lying around to hear a familiar voice, or the beating of a heart — Sei Shonagon's for example...All the galleries lead to stations, the same companies own the stores and the railroads that bear their name, Keio, Oda-kyu, all those names of ports. The train inhabited by sleeping people puts together all the fragments of a dream, makes a single film of them, the ultimate film. The tic-kets from the automatic dispenser grant admission to the show.

Video games are the first stage in a plan for machines to help the human race, the only plan that offers a future for intelli-gence. For the moment, the in-superable philosophy of our time is contained in the Pac-Man. I didn't know, when I was sacrificing all my coins to him, that he was going to conquer the world. Perhaps because he is the most perfect graphic metaphor of Man's Fate. He puts into true perspective the balance of power between the individual and the environment, and he tells us soberly that though there may be honor in carrying out the greatest number of victorious attacks, it always comes a cropper.

He was pleased that the same chrysanthemums appeared in funerals for men and for animals. He described to me the ceremony held at the zoo in Ueno, in memory of animals that had died during the year: For two years in a row this day of mourning has had a pall cast over it by the death of a panda — more irreparable, according to the newspapers, than the death of the Prime Minister that took place at the same time. Last year people really cried. Now they seem to be getting used to it, accepting that each year Death takes a panda as dragons do young girls in fairy tales. I've heard this sentence: *The partition that separates life from death does not appear so thick to us as it does to a Westerner.* What I have read most often in the eyes of people about to die is surprise. What I read right now in the eyes of Japanese children is curiosity. As if they were trying, in order to understand the death of an animal, to stare through the partition.

I have returned from a country where Death is not a partition to cross through, but a road to follow. The Great Ancestor of the Bijago archipelago has described for us the itinerary of the dead, and how they move from island to island according to a rigorous protocol, until they come to the last beach where they wait for the ship that will take them to the other world. If by accident one should meet them, it is above all imperative not to recognize them. Hayao Yamaneko invents video games with his machine. To please me, he puts in my best-beloved animals, the Cat and the Owl.

He claims that electronic texture is the only one that can deal with sentiment, memory and imagination. Mizoguchi's Arsene Lupin, for example, or the no-less imaginary Burakumin. How can one claim to show a category of Japanese who do not exist? Yet, they're there, I saw them in Osaka hiring themselves out by the day, sleeping on the ground, ever since the Middle Ages they've been doomed to grubby and backbreaking jobs, and their real name, *Etas,* is a taboo word, not to be pronounced. They are non-persons, how can they be shown, except as non-images?

The Bijagos are part of Guinea-Bissau. In an old film clip, Amilcar Cabral waves a gesture of goodbye to the shore — he's right, he'll never see it again. Luiz Cabral made the same gesture fifteen years later, on the canoe that was bringing us back. Guinea has by that time become a nation, and Luiz is its president. All those who remember the war remember him. He is the half-brother of Amilcar, born as he was of mixed Guinean and Cape Verdian blood and like him a founding member of an unusual Party, the PAIGC, which by uniting the two colonized countries in a single movement of struggle wishes to be the forerunner of a federation of the two states. I have listened to the stories of former guerilla fighters, who had fought in conditions so inhuman that they pitied the Portuguese soldiers for having to bear what they themselves suffered — that I heard, and many more things that make one ashamed for having used lightly, even inadvertently, the word guerilla to describe a certain breed of film-making...A word that at the time was linked to many theoretical debates, and also to bloody defeats on the ground. Amilcar Cabral was the only one to lead a victorious guerilla war — and not only in terms of military conquests. He knew his people, he had studied them for a long time, he wanted every liberated region to be also the precursor of a different kind of society. The socialist countries send weapons to arm the fighters, the social-democracies fill the people's stores: may the extreme Left forgive History, but if the guerillas are like fish in water, it's thanks to Sweden...Amilcar was not afraid of ambiguities, he knew the traps. He wrote: *It's as though we were at the edge of a great river full of waves and storms, with people who are trying to cross it and drown, but they have no other way out: they must get to the other side.*

And now the scene moves to Cassaca, the 17th of February 1980 — but to understand it properly one must move forward in time. In one year, Luiz Cabral the president will be in prison, and the weeping man he has just decorated, Major Nino, will have taken power. The Party will have split, Guineans and Cape Verdians separated one from another will be fighting over Amilcar's legacy. We will learn that behind this ceremony of promotions which in the eyes of visitors, perpetuated the brotherhood of the struggle, there lay a pit of post-victory bitterness, and that Nino's tears did not express an ex-warrior's emotion, but the wounded pride of a hero who felt he had not been raised high enough above the others. And beneath each of these faces, a memory, and in place of what we were told had been forged into a collective memory, a thousand memories of men who parade their personal laceration in the great wound of History...

In Portugal, raised up in its turn by the breaking wave of Bissau, Miguel Torga who had struggled all his life against the dictatorship wrote: *Every protagonist represents only himself... In place of a change in the social setting, he seeks simply, in the revolutionary act, the sublimation of his own image...* That's the way the breakers recede, and so predictably that one has to believe in a kind of amnesia of the future that History distributes, through mercy or calculation, to those whom it recruits. Amilcar murdered by members of his own party, the liberated areas fallen under the yoke of bloody petty tyrants liquidated in their turn by a central power to whose stability everyone paid hommage until the military coup. . . That's how History advances, plugging its memory as one plugs one's ears. Luiz exiled to Cuba, Nino discovering in his turn plots woven against him, can be cited reciprocally to appear before the bar of History — she doesn't care, she understands nothing, she has only one friend, the one Brando spoke of in *Apocalypse:* horror — and horror has a name and a face.

I am writing you all this from another world, a world of appearances. In a way, the two worlds communicate with each other. Memory is to one what History is to the other. An impossibility. Legends are born out of the need to decipher the indecipherable,Memories must make do with their delirium, with their drift. A moment stopped would burn like a flame of film blocked before the furnace of the projector. Madness protects, as fever does. I envy Hayao and his Zone. He plays with the signs of his memory. He pins them down and decorates them like insects that would have flown beyond Time and which he could contemplate from a point outside of Time— the only eternity we have left. I look at his machines, I think of a world where each memory could create its own legend.

In Iceland, I laid the first stone of an imaginary film. That summer, I had met three children on a road, and a volcano had come out of the sea. . . The American astronauts came to train, before flying off to the Moon, in this corner of Earth that resembles it, I saw it immediately as a setting for science-fiction, the landscape of another planet. . . or rather no, let it be the landscape of our own planet for someone who comes from elsewhere, from very far away. I imagine him moving slowly, heavily, about the volcanic soil that sticks to the soles. All of a sudden, he stumbles, and the next step, it is a year later, he is walking on a small path near the Dutch border, along a seabird's sanctuary.

That's for a start. Now why this cut in time, this connection of memories? That's just it, *he* can't understand. He hasn't come from another planet, he comes from our future. 4001, the time when the human brain has reached the era of full employment. Everything works to perfection, all that *we* allow to slumber, including memory. Logical consequence: total recall is memory anesthetized. After so many stories of men who had lost their memory, here is the story of one who has lost forgetting. . . and who, through some peculiarity of his nature, instead of drawing pride from the fact and scorning mankind of the past and its shadows, turned to it first with curiosity and then with compassion. In the world he comes from, to call forth a vision, to be moved by a portrait, to tremble at the sound of music can only be signs of a long and painful prehistory. He wants to understand. He feels these infirmities of Time like an injustice, and he reacts to that injustice like Che Guevara, like the youth of the Sixties, with indignation. He is a third-worlder of Time, the idea that unhappiness had existed in his planet's past is as unbearable to him as to them the existence of poverty in their present.

Naturally, he will fail. The unhappiness he discovers is as inaccessible to him as the poverty of a poor country is unimaginable to the children of a rich one. He has chosen to give up his privileges, but he can do nothing about the privilege that has allowed him to choose. His only recourse is precisely that which threw him into this absurd quest: a song cycle by Moussorgski. They are still sung in the 40th century. Their meaning has been lost, but it was then that for the first time he perceived the presence of that thing he did not understand, which had something to do with unhappiness and memory, and towards which, slowly, heavily, he began to walk.

On may 15th, 1945, at 7 o'clock in the morning, the 382nd US Infantry Regiment attacked a hill in Okinawa they had renamed *Dick Hill.* I suppose the Americans themselves believed they were conquering Japanese soil, and that they knew nothing about Ryukyu civilization. Neither did I, apart from the fact that the faces of the market ladies at Itoman spoke to me more of Gauguin than of Utamaro. For centuries of dreamy vassalage, Time had not moved in the archipelago. Then came the break. Is it a property of islands to make their women into the guardians of their memory? I learned that, as in the bijagos, it is through the women that magic knowledge is transmitted: each community has its priestess, the Noro, who presides over all ceremonies, with the exception of funerals. The Japanese defended their position inch by inch, at the end of the day the two half-platoons formed from the remnants of L company had got only halfway up the hill. A hill like the one where I followed a group of villagers on their way to the purification ceremony. The Noro communicates with the gods of the sea, of the rain, of the earth, of fire. Everyone bows down before the Sister Deity who is the reflection, in the absolute, of a privileged relationship between brother and sister. Even after her death, the sister maintains her spiritual predominance. At dawn, toppled into the modern world. Twenty-seven years of American occupation, the re-establishment of a controversial Japanese sov-ereignty, two miles from the bowling alleys and the gas stations the Noro continues her dialogue with the gods. When she is gone, the dialogue will end. Brothers will no longer know that their dead sister is watching over them.

When filming this cere-mony, I knew I was present at the end of something. Magical cul-tures that disappear leave traces to those who succeed them. This one will leave none. The break in history has been too violent. I touch-ed that break at the summit of the hill, as I had touched it at the edge of the ditch where 200 girls had used grenades to commit suicide in 1945, rather than fall alive into the hands of Americans. People have their pictures taken in front of the ditch, as souvenirs.

On Hayao's machine, war resembles letters being burned, shredded in a frame of fire, the code name for Pearl Harbor was *Tora, tora, tora:* the name of the cat the couple in Go To Ku Ji was praying for. So all of this will have begun with the name of a cat pronounced three times.

Off Okinawa, kamikazes dived on the American fleet. They would become a legend. They were likelier material for it, obviously, than the special units who exposed their prisoners to the bitter first of Manchuria and then to hot water, so as to see how fast flesh separates from the bone. One would have to read their last letters to know that the kamikazes weren't all volunteers, nor were they all swashbuckling samurais. Before drinking his last cup of sake, Ryoji Uebara had written: *I have always thought that Japan must live free in order to live eternally. It may seem idiotic to say that today, under a totalitarian regime. We kamikaze pilots are machines, we have nothing to say, except to beg our compatriots to make Japan the great country of our dreams. In the plane I am a machine, a bit of magnetized metal that will plaster itself on an aircraft-carrier, but once on the ground, I'm a human being, with feelings and passions. . . Please excuse these disorganized thoughts. I am leaving you a rather melancholy picture, but in the depths of my heart I am happy. I have spoken frankly. Forgive me.*

Everytime he came back from Africa, he stopped at the Island of Sal, which is in fact a salt rock in the middle of the Atlantic. At the end of the island, beyond the village of Santa Maria and its cemetery with the painted tombs, it suffices to walk straight ahead to meet the desert.

He wrote me: I've understood the visions. Suddenly, you're in the desert the way you are in the night. Whatever is not desert no longer exists. You don't want to believe the images that crop up.

Did I write you that there are emus in the Ile de France: this name, Island of France, sounds strangely on the Island of Sal. My memory superimposes two towers, the one at the ruined castle of Montepilloy that served as an encampment for Joan of Arc, and the lighthouse tower at the southern tip of Sal, probably one of the last lighthouses to use oil.

A lighthouse in the Sahel looks like a collage until you see the ocean at the edge of the sand and salts. Crews of transcontinental planes are rotated on Sal. Their club brings to this frontier of nothingness a small touch of the seaside resort which makes the picture still more unreal. They feed the stray dogs that live on the beach.

I found my dogs pretty nervous tonight. They were playing with the sea as I had never seen them before. Listening to Radio Hong Kong later on, I understood: today was the first day of the lunar new year, and for the first time in sixty years, the sign of the dog met the sign of Water.

Out there, 11,000 miles away, a single shadow remains immobile in the midst of the long moving shadows that the January light throws over the ground of Tokyo: the shadow of the Asakusa bonze.

For also in Japan, the Year of the dog is beginning. Temples are filled with visitors who come to toss down their coins and to pray, Japanese style: a prayer which slips into life without interrupting it.

Brooding at the end of the world, on my Island of Sal, in the company of my prancing dogs, I remember that month of January in Tokyo, or rather I remember the images I filmed of the month of January in Tokyo. They have substituted themselves for my memory, they *are* my memory. I wonder how people remember things who don't film, don't photograph, don't tape. How has mankind managed to remember . . . I know, it wrote the Bible. The new Bible will be an eternal magnetic tape of a Time that will have to reread itself constantly, just to know it existed. As we await the year 4001 and its total recall, that's what the oracles we take out of their long hexagonal boxes at New Year may offer us: a little more power over that memory that runs from camp to camp, like Joan of Arc, that a shortwave announcement from Hong Kong Radio picked up on a Cape Verde Island projects to Tokyo, and that the memory of a precise color in the street bounces back on another country, another distance, another music, endlessly.

At the end of memory's path, the ideograms of the Island of France are no less enigmatic than the kanji of Tokyo, in the miraculous light of the New Year. It's Indian Winter. As if the air were the first element to emerge purified from the countless ceremonies by which the Japanese wash off one year to enter the next one. A full month is just enough for them to fulfill all the duties that courtesy owes to time. The most interesting unquestionably being the acquisition, at the temple of Tenjin, of the Uso bird who, according to one tradition, eats all your lies of the year to come, and according to another, turns them into truths.

But what gives the street its color in January, what makes it suddenly different, is the appearance of kimonos. In the street, in stores, in offices, even at the Stock Exchange on opening day, the girls take out their fur-collared winter kimonos. At that moment of the year other Japanese may well invent extra-flat TV sets, commit suicide with a chain saw or capture two-thirds of the world market for semi-conductors — good for them! All you see are the girls.

The 15th of January is Coming-of-Age day, an obligatory celebration in the life of a young Japanese woman. The city governments distribute small bags filled with gifts, date-books, advice: how to be a good citizen, a good mother, a good wife. On that day, every twenty year old girl can phone her family for free, no matter where in Japan. Flag, home and country, this is the anteroom of adulthood. The world of the Takenoko and of rock singers speeds away like a rocket. Speakers explain what society expects of them. How long will they take to forget the Secret?

And when all the celebrations are over, it remains only to pick up all the ornaments, all the accessories of the celebration, and by burning them, make a celebration.

This is Dondo-yaki. A Shinto blessing of the debris that has a right to immortality, like the dolls at Ueno. The last stage, before their disappearance, of the poignancy of things. Daruma the one-eyed spirit reigns supreme at the summit of the bonfire. Abandonment must be a feast, laceration must be a feast, and the farewell to all that one has lost, broken, used, must be enobled by a ceremony. It's Japan that could fulfill the wish of that french writer who wanted divorce to be made a sacrament. The only baffling part of this ritual was the circle of children striking the ground with their long poles. I only got one explanation—a singular one, although for me it might take the form of a small intimate service: it was to chase away the moles.

And that's where my three children of Iceland came and grafted themselves in. I picked up the whole shot again, adding the somewhat hazy end, the frame trembling under the force of the wind beating us down on the cliff, everything I had cut in order to "tidy up" and that said better than all the rest what I saw in that moment, why I held it at arm's length, at zoom's length, until its last 24th of a second...The city of Heimaey spread out below us, and when, five years later, my friend Haroun Tazieff sent me the film he had just shot in the same place, I lacked only the name to learn that nature performs its own Dondo-yakis. The island's volcano had awakened. I looked at those pictures, and it was as if the entire year '65 had just been covered with ashes.

So it sufficed to wait, and the planet itself staged the working of Time. I saw what had been my window again, I saw emerge familiar roofs and balconies, the landmarks of the walks I took through town every day, down to the cliff where I had met the children. The cat with white socks that Haroun had been considerate enough to film for me naturally found its place, and I thought that of all the prayers to Time that had studded this trip, the kindest was the one spoken by the woman of Go To Ku Ji who said simply to her cat Tora: *Cat, wherever you are, peace be with you.*

And then in its turn, the journey entered the Zone. Hayao showed me my images already affected by the moss of Time, freed of the lie that had prolonged the existence of those moments swallowed by the Spiral.

from 'Sans Soleil', courtesy of New Yorker Films

Naked Needle

Nuruddin Farah

It would be a very good idea, I think, if I took you round the wonderful city of Mogadiscio and showed you the treasures as well as the hidden infirmities of this ancient African settlement. Perhaps we shall be tired, both of us, before we see much of it, since I must drop in at my friend's place, my friend, whom, I imagine, I presume, you will immediately be fond of, and with whom, if you wish, that is *only if you wish,* you will be able to stay for the night. My friend, who is a mulatta, will feel grateful, I am sure, and, as I have said, will be more than pleased to put you up overnight. I cannot take you to my place, I cannot, and much though I wish to avoid it, I must mention that in my little room geckos live side by side with the spirits of my ancestors who call on me in the early mornings and evenings; and I am afraid the ugly sight of the ants, black and white, their slow movements up and down the walls that are plastered with their droppings, the geckos' bouncing on the flies that are trapped in the spider webs up the naked ceiling, all this, my Nancy, may give you more than a nightmare. Not to forget, of course, the mosquitoes of the bull-breed that buzz into your ears. So, whenever I have a visitor, a date, or a personality, a personality of your taste, Nancy, I take them elsewhere, send them elsewhere. that is. My belongings are, strange as it may sound, all packed up in my suitcase, the case is still intact, labelled ALITALIA, ROME—MOGADISCIO, un-opened, so to speak, just as I flew in.

Come, Nancy, please come, and let us together discover the calamity, the er . . . *eternity* of this city that has a divinity of its own kind, let us climb over the Hadrian's Wall in order that we may have the pleasure, in order that we may have a closer look at it. Let us talk about Mogadiscio, the city that has fascinated foreigners as well as the locals with the beauty of its name. We shall walk and walk and take our sweet time, we shall see and stop, if need be, we shall ask people things I know nothing about, if necessary, we shall go to a snack-bar if we are hungry, and we shall take a taxi on our way back, and, if you wish, we shall take a walk back, provided there is enough time to go to that party that we've been invited to through Mohamed and Barbara. Give your hand to me, Nancy, in the name of heaven give, let me take your hand, and I shall lead you through the gate and protect you from the dog, Barbara's dog that rises from its daily slumber with the setting of the sun. How I hated dogs when I was abroad, Nancy. Dogs, how I hated dogs that protected wives of jealous husbands, dogs that were tied to poles near gates, not to protect the proprietor, neither to propitiate the husband's jealous instincts, but to deaden the erotic instincts of Don Giovannis. A dog bit me in the leg when I was in London and ever since that time, I've been scared shit of them. That is it, your arm. The mood, woman, change your mood, *revolutionize* yourself, and smile to the infant twilight, and, please, take your pleasure in watching, with gratitude to the gods, watch with abundant affection, the sucked-out blood of the day's dead up in the blue, clear sky in the western sphere. In the meanwhile, we shall both join, in our hearts, in lamenting, we shall join the wailing of the silent mourners. Rise to your feet, I cannot pull you up, you are heavy, Nancy. Rise, on your own.

That is Bar Warder, named, I don't know why, after a small but important town in the Somali Territory under Ethiopian Administration. One and a half million Somalis under Ethiopian Administration. They are robbed, they are killed, their women are raped, and they are political under-dogs. Yes, Nancy, under-dogs. And Bar Warder, the bar that has been named after that small town in the Ethiopian plains, is about the ...er...most famous teashop in the city, famous for the excellent local music they play to entertain their customers who never consume more than a cup of spiced tea at the most and who sit almost all night and idly chat about politics in the Middle East and Vietnam, in fact, about any political mishaps in any part of the world. And that is...

What is this?
The Proletariat Palace.
And the emblem?
The Proletariat's
How interesting.
Recently constructed, just a month ago.
Impressive.

And that is Teatro So- 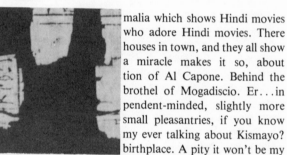 malia which shows Hindi movies women-folk and the children-folk who adore Hindi movies. There are, I think, about fifteen movie houses in town, and they all show flicks about horse wranglers or, a miracle makes it so, about rough-hewn robbers in the tradi- tion of Al Capone. Behind the cinema building is the famous big brothel of Mogadiscio. Er...in Kismayo, Nancy, people are inde- pendent-minded, slightly more frivolous and...enjoy life's small pleasantries, if you know what I mean. Do you remember my ever talking about Kismayo? Yes, you do. Wonderful. It is my birthplace. A pity it won't be my burial place, most likely, I am afraid I have a feeling I shall not die there. At any rate, I was in Kismayo about two months ago, and I hated the place. Too much foreign influence. Because girls turn spinsters before their teens just like in Mogadiscio and they scoot towards their downfall, with a mind to relate their experiences, narrate it in the style of a saga to the dust unto which they will return. Prostitution in Somalia, Nancy, is at one's doorstep, and little milk-teethed tarts are saddled (and mentally fastened) to seats in cars; the fledgelings are picked up on the curbs free of charge, for a packet of Benson and Hedges and a ride in the car will quiet their roaring nerves. God's curse on us all, amen.

Red lights, Nancy, stop. Red, *red,* can't you see? That is Xawo Tacco, the first Somali woman martyr. An arrow, can't you see the arrow piercing just below her breasts? She was in the Jihad against the Italian infidels, and a Somali, whose son is now govenor of a region, hit her. The arrow was poisoned, and she died of it. Still red, don't move.

I AM NOT COLOUR-BLIND, Koschin!
Yolk of an egg, why is it yellow?
How do I know?
Why are the Chinese the most productive of the human race, and the Indians?
How should I know.
Green in the traffic light, and in flags—what does it symbolize?

I don't know, Koschin. YOU ARE HURTING ME, darling!
I got excited, sorry.
It's all right, darling!
Red symbolizes the mens-period of women, red symbolizes 'family-planning'.
And green?
Fertile land, after menstruation is over.
And yellow?
The act of flirting with your car in place of women. Red you stand by, yellow you flirt, and green you go in.
That's wonderful.

Affair-Irdood, where the four streets of old meet, is down this road, and that is the noisiest place ever. For there is the African market, and you will remember so many places you have seen elsewhere in Africa. And this other road leads you to Electricity House, a property nationalized a year or so ago. Used to belong to an Italian, it was handed down to his wife, a Somali. But, Nancy, the Russians, with all their political piracy have agreed to construct a dam, Fanoole Dam, at Fanoole. Jaalle Siyad went to Moscow and signed the contract. A dam, Nancy, with canals and a hydro-power station including some agricultural equipment to come along with the first install-ment of the aid. Russians know how to sing their own praises, as Dawn has said. Whereas the Chinese, Nancy, are a very honest people. That dam...

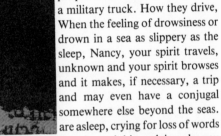

Nancy, watch out, there's a military truck. How they drive, reckless and inattentive. Yes. When the feeling of drowsiness or exhaustion *takes over you,* you drown in a sea as slippery as the surface of a snake. And when you sleep, Nancy, your spirit travels, with lightning speed, into the unknown and your spirit browses over unseen and ancestor spirits, and it makes, if necessary, a trip of more than a thousand miles, and may even have a conjugal relationship with another spirit somewhere else beyond the seas. Your mouth waters while you are asleep, crying for loss of words over the pain of parting. You talk in your sleep, Nancy, and soliloquize and this explains why you are at times unsatisfied with your sleep. And you suffer from insomnia whenever your spirit is ostracized from the nucleus of the family-spirits in which it belongs and your spirit refuses to depart *from* you and you feel heavy, deadly and dead-like. Death descends...Dead? Dead-like? Deadly.

Death descends upon us from nowhere as if we have disobeyed a certain code of behaviour. The irony of the matter is that the dying, and their relatives, think that they will go straight to heaven, which is, in my opinion, a misconceived conception of a reality — the reality of the Next World. For heaven is neither up nor is it down nor is it before the Judgement. Heaven is neither lukewarm, of tepid temper...what I am saying? The path outstretched to test the walking ability of the passers is not situated on top of a bridge which is in the lowest pit of Gehenna; this bridge is not as sharp as a sword. But the rollcall and the Judgement are all antecedents to the blowing of the bugle which is preceded by the epicentrum. Those who laugh a little here in this Vanishing World cry a lot in the Next Everlasting World, it is said. The curtain is drawn, the labeling is done with, checked and re-checked, and the final registration is completed. Time in the Next World is a long expansion of nothingness and everythingness with no dimensions, no days, no nights, not even a change of climate. *Is this the old part of the city?*

Body Fluids (and other mobile homes)

Gregory Whitehead

Speed is in the air, and it should be clear to all of us that the human body is well behind the times. As the means of extinction accelerate, the body remains its old, sluggish self. Are we fluid or are we jam? What follows is a dossier of documents pertaining to the broad research: Might not species history best be written as the history of the body in its desperate attempts to keep the pace?

Testimony (c. 1950) You ask me that as if there's something wrong with me. I love my mobile home, I love it because it's mobile and because it's my home, *our* home, a home for me and my family. My husband was a member of a tank crew during the war until he lost a hand near Brest. The VA was good to us, and he was a good soldier. They gave us our mobile home, it used to be some kind of mobile command 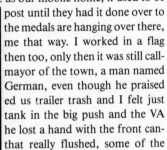 post until they had it done over to live in. And we're not trailer trash, the medals are hanging over there, so don't you go about looking at me that way. I worked in a flag factory. I lived in a mobile home, then too, only then it was still call- ed a trailer, and even though the mayor of the town, a man named Brommer or Bruner, something German, even though he praised our patriotic duty, they still call- ed us trailer trash and I felt just like a carnie. My husband drove tank in the big push and the VA gave us this mobile home when he lost a hand with the front can- non jamming. We have a toilet that really flushed, some of the others don't flush, they're just drop holes to a septic tank. Since then, we've moved three times. The first was when the flag plant was closed, they told us that with the war over, the flags weren't flying, so they said thanks and we were both out of a job. My husband lost a hand in the war, so he can't work but gets good disability. For a while, a lot of us kept living around the plant, it was empty and just stared at us, then I *did* feel like part of a circus caravan circled around the big top too long after the crowd's gone home. So we moved a ways north and I started to work at a truck stop, just a walk away. Truckers know what it's like, I never heard a bad word about trailers from a trucker. You can move, you're light, you follow the jobs and it doesn't swallow all you make, those swamplands suburbs aren't for me. We don't owe a cent on this, and it's made of finest aluminum. But then I got pregnant, that's another story, and there was no school, no community, I mean something more than a fast park by the turnpike. We heard about trailer parks springing up and that people, all kinds of people, were buying mobile homes. And that's what we had, so we just hooked up and moved to a park outside of Scranton. It was real convenient because Chuck could just about walk to town and pick up his check and trade war stories and I got a job right away in a better place, a lounge near one of the very first shopping malls, in Pennsylvania at least. The last time, to this place, was just three months ago. They were advertising in all the papers, all kinds of facilities, very modern, very clean. Well it wasn't all they said, but it suits us fine. Some of the women have their hands full here, and for a little extra, they'll watch the kids for you. Chuck does what he can, but you know he lost a hand in the war and gets kind of down sometimes. He doesn't mean to, but he gets a little violent and even though we like it here for the most part we're not gypsies and it's kind of small and we all have to bust loose. All the friends we have in the world are right here. Yeah, we feel separate but we get by.

Keynote Address (c. 1959) Gentlemen, let us begin with the human body. If you will observe the specimen to your left, the Good Worker Schmidt, you will notice several outstanding qualities. In some ways, he represents everything we could have hoped for. He has worked hard and consumed avidly. He shops and votes responsibly and often. He responds well to incentives and has accepted his career limitations. He sees unions as a threat to his independence and an office job as a threat to his heritage. So what, you are asking, is the problem? Most of you would hire Schmidt on the spot. And in doing so, I suggest you would be putting yourselves into a bit of a jam. For you see, gentlemen, for all his surface virtues, Good Worker Schmidt is stuck. Or, to put it differently, the lubricant for his orderly exertions is at the same time the quickly hardening cement for his innermost obstinancies.

I have with me here on the lecturn a quart of Schmidt's sweat. Examine just a few drops beneath a microscope and you will begin to understand what I am getting at. In the full clarity of magnification, you will see that Schmidt belongs to a bowling league, a rotary club, he performs his civic duty, he grows tomatoes in window boxes — and his tomatoes must be tended. Schmidt doesn't like to travel, vacation means a two week hunker with a firm family grapple hook. The problem is smeared all over the slide, gentle- men; *stick* with Schmidt and you'll soon be *stuck* with Schmidt.

While it is not my inten- tion to lecture you on the funda- mentals of good economics, one simple point bears repeating. If the labor market is to function perfectly, that is, if it is to remain in a condition of perfect fluidity, that is, the absence of friction, then the fundamental datum to which I must always return is the *human body,* a liquid item to be sure but also that most conspic- uous repository, a generator even, for every conceivable friction. It's the body of fluids, of juices, of lubrication that we must learn to distill away from the other body, the *basic* body, that heavy flesh that simmers with all those wearisome questions of what is to be *done* with the juices, of where to *propel* the juices, of the most propitious way to *carry* them, well, all this must be put to an *end,* we cannot let the metallic body of efficient production become too attached to the fluid body of the market! Here's the point: detachment from space, the economy of separation, there lies the key to the perfectly fluid labor market, that is the labor market, the *only* labor market, that can keep up with capital, for we all know that capital is on the move, it cannot be stopped, we are constantly tabulating in arrears as we juggle our stubborn flesh, and they are not the same, *but we must will it so.*

Gentlemen, I need not remind you that the de facto post-war advantages we have enjoyed over the past decade are coming to a close. There are already unmistakable signs from West Germany and Japan that they are learning to put the economies of obliteration to good use, they no longer have such cumbersome gunnysacks full of history and I warn you they will soon be on our heels. War made them fluid at the same time it made us fat and attached. They are left with such a marvelously clear slate while we sit among whole suburbs full of Schmidts!

I'll be frank with you. If we cannot succeed in prying Schmidt loose from the obstinate concreta of his physical shell, we will all soon be watching our most precious fat, that is to say our *profits,* dripping away into his barbecue pit. At the risk of repeating myself, the problem with Schmidt is not in his performance motivation but in his physical immobility. Further, what is

46

keeping Schmidt stuck is not going to change overnight. How then, to find a way to keep Schmidt solid but at the same time *make him flow?*

Well, I suggest to you that the most feasible way to melt Schmidt down is not to turn up the heat but to bolt on wheels. Yes, gentlemen, I call your attention to a most magnificent labor market lubricant that has the supreme virtue of already existing, an aluminum solution to Schmidt's heaviest mettle, an optimal site for the optimal mixmastering of labor and capital, a place where the two reside in a single, calculable, predictable, collapsible unit, a place where living labor can live, flow, percolate, call it home or call it capitalopolis. What I am talking about, gentlemen, is the MOBILE HOME.

Confession (c. 1968)   I have news for you; and a confession to make.

I am the trash motif that fills your nightmare world.

I am an automohobo, I latch onto any old angst that comes my way.

Make no mistake — my ongoing movement is not footloose. I'm a parasite and I feed off the land, off your land, your every turf is an open graze, fast food feed to my triple wide mouth.

You've been looking for me, haven't you. You've been looking *at* me, haven't you? And why not, I begin the day with a morning peel, strip back the Reynolds Wrap for a manicure a la mooche. Just last week, I turned my readymade dishwasher into a fish tank for guppies and blow mouth scavengers of an unclassified genus. A little later, I'll scrape the snails from my concrete underslabs and have a happy feast, while I make my plans, while I answer your questions, while I spread the plague and threaten to get a move on — again.

I am the gypsy; am I the gypsy who feeds off the fear that I might be a gypsy, that I might be on the loose, that I might be unattached, that I might have no-where to go but *your* place, that my body might wriggle into quarters unexpected, that it might melt a bit, leave a residue that won't wash? My clothes are cut from factory installed draperies; they itch me so furiously, I rock my wheel estate wooly, won't you join me? When I tire of your fretful sluices, I chew the stuffing from my readymade couch, my readymade stools, my readymade bedroom set, yours is next, are you ready for me?

There are others like me. We are the refuse of trailer parks, the shambles round the war plant. We built your nuclear reactors and your super-hardened peace-keeping bric-a-brac not because we had to but because we find your titanic wastes so very tasty, wrapped as they are in finest flagstaff linen. You see, we are the surplus that wouldn't sit still, we picked up after the great dumping and started on our way, we're so fluid we can't be counted — so you call us dirty dark trailer trash.

As the pastor of tarmac parking lots, I have nothing to fear. I can appear in your laundry bag, in your trashmasher, in your septic tank, in your memory bank. Fess up — where *are* you most dirty? That is where I'm going next. I confess. I am a mobile dump site. I am a cankersore, the peels you see on the outside of my rig are chancres, cast in Alcoa's finest. In time, I've learned to live on your wastes, though the real pleasure comes from deeding you mine. Sooner or later, it all comes out on the skin, tar and feathers. Won't you let me play my fetid organs for you, sweetly?

Last month, I converted my toilet into a suction cup that sucks along through your dirtiest places, the spaces that feed me, sucking it all up and spilling it forth into my double-wide living room pick-through plant. Here's where I decide to nibble, ferment or transport the whole mess to another town, to a church, a bingo parlor or a kindergarten. I am poison; once in jest, I fed a toxic copy of *Travels With Charley* to a hungry building inspector. Appetite Americana, can't you find it?

Slowly my mobile home, my Rollohome, strips down to a tin can carbuncle. I challenge your most skillful social surgeons to flush me out. I long to feel your scalpels probing through the fleshy folds of my dwelling unit. Won't you come in for another chat, for some cooling fluids? You look concerned, but there's really nothing to be done. I am an externality, a side effect, a diseconomy, an exogene. I make my bed among your refusals; here lies the secret pleasure of an industrialized parasite. But you know that I keep my word, that before winter next I will have eaten my mobile home inside out, it will be thoroughly digested as the icon of your stability and all that you own will be my fair game.

I do confess — my lips have never smacked more fully. Bon appetit!

Excerpt (c. 1986)   Expended much of the day staring at my collection of photographs taken from the body politic, giving me a strange and not entirely cerebral pleasure. I feel myself shrink at the sight of so many folds, at the way they glisten at the slightest exertion, sweating and shuddering in an excess of democracy. The most recent aerial glossies from the Urban Commission are particularly revealing. Is it my appetite or my science that makes me inspect so fervently? Always the same: The politicians expect their simple answers while my moist eyes roll along surfaces of public parts they never even see.

Late this evening, I experienced eyestrain and asthmatic fits, so I put away the photos and scan the reports. Page after page of standard deviations and parabolic curves — as if the body politic could be cut and dried, a nifty mannequin for the lads in the think tank! There are no *fluids* in these reports, no sense of *wetness*, that is what upsets me, obsesses me. They operate with the mentality of a tailor, as if the state and consistency of political flesh were everywhere the same.

Unable to sleep. Head spinning with the same old dilemma. Cast the body in concrete and face the problem of politics, enthusiastic exercise of rights that has plagued us so unmercifully over the past several years. But enhance fluidity and the whole mess becomes thoroughly incalculable, impossible to count, hence predict. Whenever we dry the body out, we get pressure from the private sector — *Things are too stiff, we want our human capital to behave like bank transfers, liquid assets!* And then when we try to get the body moving a bit, just a prod here and a prod there, well, then we find *ourselves* in a jam. Ach!

After breakfast, I pulled the file on the mobile home experiments. Here was supposed to be the answer, *hard fluidity,* a metallic wetness to make the labor market a comfy, homey place to slide around in, the softest conceivable casing for the hardest facts of marginal competitive advantage. And it was all ours, singularly American, designed to run rings around the Japanese model. Even today, after so many years, I cringe at the remembrance of the result, what *happens* to people when they're on the move like that, plugging in to the location theorist's clever topography, the filth, the tax chaos, the mass parasitism, slime you could shine. . .

This afternoon, I endeavored to prepare my final report. I know full well the politicians prefer design to anatomy. They could never understand what I have seen over these long months of ashing through social flows and pourings, they won't even get their feet wet. They just don't have the juice for my real results, so I cooked up a bare fact conclusion that will put me out of the probe for good:

*Speed brings filth into motion and motion into politics. The only way to pulse the social body and keep it corpus, the only way to make the economy of movement balance out against the miseries of flesh-on-the loose, is to make a circuit of circulation. The only truly **clean** motion is electronic, and **that**, my dear colleagues, is out of my field.*

Traffic Report (c. 1982) Symbolically and financially, the Triboro Bridge was situated at the heart of the Robert Moses intra-urban arterial system. Beneath its massive concrete support columns, Moses was to build the master bunker Bridge and Tunnel Authority that would serve as his administrative headquarters for the following quarter century. On opening day—July 11, 1936—the bridge itself was almost universally cheered as one of civil engineering's most remarkable achievements. A month later, on August 17, 1936, the bridge was put to a battery acid test; everyone in upper Manhattan decided more or less at the same time that a day on Jones Beach would be good for their circulation. The ensuing traffic snarl was described by many as the worst in the history of the city. Moses' intricate apparatus for sorting, tolling and conveying, the World's Largest Artificial Heart, had turned into one enormous clot. The solution? To Robert Moses, King of Jam, the answer was obvious: another bridge.

Speed brings motion into politics; each acceleration of traffic is accompanied by an infusion of circulation space with political power. As the Moseleum meant traffic on an unprecedented scale, and as Moses never ceased being a champion of the fast lane, his plan served as a vast repository of power over the most decisive years in the shaping of the New York built environment. Over half a century, that power was frozen into tarmac and concrete. The Moseleum was designed to survive its inhabitants. With each anniversary of his death, Moses commemoration is automatic — the plan is all around us, in every honk, in every jam.

Within sight of the laboring Triboro pump, where the LIE meets the BQE meets the Grand Central meets La Guardia near Shea, the open wound Moseleum reveals an inner sanctum, a ruin without crumble, tons of coliseum concrete looming over Flushing Meadow. The New York State Pavilion was designed as a home team centerpiece for the 1964 World's Fair under the signature of three Very Big Men: Moses, Philip Johnson and Nelson Rockefeller.

This megamanmonument, with its sixteen massive columns, three Big Boy observation towers, wire-rope rigging and vinyl panels, was also billed as the World's Largest Tent. In a fair featuring king size (the World's Largest Rubber Tire, the World's Biggest Cheese and so on), it is hardly surprising that Moses should rise to the occasion with such a spectacular outpouring of sement. But the World's Largest **Tent?**

The Moses Pavilion is a Johnson Speer, built for a time when nothing budges. This is not to say that it is empty; against the white noise backdrop of everywhere traffic, the pedestrian visitor can hear the fluttering of wings. Given Philip Johnson's exceptional talent for architectural scavenging, is it not appropriate that the pavement pavilion should become, at last, the world's largest pigeon roost?

No matter. There will come a time when outside, all mechanical mobility will have wound down into myth. Inside, the collected heirs of extinction will wander across the Texaco terrazo of the World's Largest Map thinking, oh, so **this** was territory. And deep within the columns of this ancient traffic shrine will be found an oracle, an oracle devoted to Homo Statis, an oracle recounting manifold stories of Stonehenge in Flushing, of the time when power was said to reside either in cinder blocks or electro-signals, when absolute speed was discovered to be equivalent to absolute impenetrability, when all the world buzzed with debates over super-hardness and satellites, when the prophets spread the last word for the last time: DIG IN OR BEAM OUT!

Eulogy (c. 1998)   *Body fluids, wither without.* Those were his final words, a last transmission cast as its own confirmation, for at the very moment of his expiration utterance, with all of medical science hovering inches above his rima glottidis,we in the observation gallery watched with dismay as his precious larynx flaked away like so much baked flounder. As the whole of his trachea crumbled beneath the urgent apparatus of nursing and inspection that descended with such authority around the remnants of his throat, I recalled another scene, years ago, standing in his library, surrounded by all the books of his life. He was stooped over, frantically poring over volume after volume, searching, or so he said, for a single speck of blood. *Where has it all run?* he asked frantically. The ink was dry, all his first love textuality had turned to brittle parchment. On that occasion, he still had the juice to weep against my shoulder, confessing nightly visions of a vast internal archive covered with dust, choking the spirit. This was just the beginning, for a week later I received a call from the hospital informing me that our beloved friend had eaten and digested the six thousand some odd volumes of his library. I rushed to his bedside, expecting the worse, only to find him smiling and happy, his stomach, in fact his entire digestive tract, stretched so enormously that the folds filled the room like a sadly deflated air bag. Now, he announced, he was prepared for his lifelong crusade: the pitting of his own united fluids against textual dessication.

Body Fluids, wither without. A confirmation, but also an admission. For though I knew his real hunger was for raw flesh, he always began each day by stuffing his esophagus with the largest granite monolith in popular memory. *Put it down to wetness!* he would say gleefully, swallowing with an alarmingly long shudder. I remember one such breakfast that featured the head of a Harpy perched on the drum of an antique printing press. He scarfed it down whole, choked, coughed up a chisel and before morning next, he had crafted himself a marvelous tray of mnemonic petit-fours.

Well, as you all know, two years ago he beamed out. It began when he sliced open his throat with a brand new razor blade and plugged his corniculates into a wall socket. When the doctors came for him, he fought them off, repeatedly shouting *ELECTROTRACHEOTOMY IS THE ORDER TODAY.* This was to remain his manifesto right up to the last hour. Clinically, they classified him as an addenoid schizophonic. In the popular press, he was branded a monster, a Gorgon of the Glottis, an Automat-Epiglot, a Laryngahobo and so on. But can any of us who knew him well think for a moment it could have been otherwise? When the chance came to actually channel his blood into the possibility of becoming absolutely oral, how could he resist? Wasn't this intermingling of the fluids of his intracorporeal mobility with the fluid of primary orality a realization of his innermost fantasy? And is it so very shocking? Anyway, in the conquest of his private utopia, his larynx was quick to become legendary. When I saw his formidable equipment molder before my eyes, I felt my own juices surge in mourning.

Body Fluids, wither without. An admission, but also a warning, For, as he would frequently remind us, while Life is the motion of juices spilling over, of words that get away, of forbidden moistures seeping into forbidden places, History is solid, fashioned counterfactually from carnage that gets stuck in the throat. *Life is the body running out of juices running into history run-*

ning dry. And so, with every subsequent triumph of the disembodied Word, with every fresh release from burden of his scriptostigma, he trembled at the curse of a time when the swollen arteries of electrofluidity would crackle with the circuitry of autodessication on a grand scale.

Body fluids, wither without.

Mistake

Unica Zürn

Without a womb, she executes the birth of a city. All the people in the airplane look at her but she is too busy with the birth of her city to see anybody. She listens: Everything through the ear is more believable than visual experience.

I want to witness, the thin man thinks, in his country, in his armchair. If there are no witnesses nobody will believe it.

Soon one will see his mad circus act in the sky. The hero in the airplane that is totally black, with a small white circle—the plane without any nationality—he will come. He gives her his hand — she jumps. That's easy and now she is ready for everything. Her courage is incredible. She! who is always so shy: That's new. After all that time — something new!

And she is certain: The steward is, at the same time, the young book-dealer, the nicest in all Paris. He gives her—free of charge—a blue pack of cagarettes. AVEC LES FELICITATIONS DE L'AIR FRANCE. It is printed on the package. The hero in the black airplane fails to come close — it is too difficult. O.k.! The party will start on another page. For she knows: Everything that will come is the greatest party in her life. *I don't think that hyp- nosis is possible from such a great distance,* says the doctor from Essen in the airplane. *But if it should be possible then the man is a criminal.* The thin man, in his country, in his armchair, gives his pleasant message: the chief of the fifth column dresses in black and white. One eats the red and the white.

In the lobby of the Frankfurt airport she sits next to a white vase. The only black object in the lobby is an iron metal-stand. It looks like a cage. *Come in,* says the thin man, in his country, in his arm-chair, and she turns into a snake. The thin man has a tiny, amused smile. *She is mad, certainly,* says the doctor who looks at her in the lobby, like all the others. *That has nothing to do with hypnosis through empty space, it is simply a crisis of madness.* She remains in the coat-stand prison and a man in blue arrives: *Come, your plane to Berlin is waiting. Give me the password!* (He doesn't understand a thing.) *Give me the password! A letter, a number. . .* And slowly he says *U–L–M–3–something. Come!* She gets up immediately. She follows him in full confidence because of the letter M. *Keep off the letter M,* had been the word of the gypsy in Palavas who had read her palm. The art dealer from Berlin and the doctor from Essen look at her as she boards the plane to Berlin. Doctor: *Her misfortune started in Paris. She doesn't eat anymore, she doesn't sleep anymore, and she is giving birth to a city. She is on her way to a loony bin. Be quiet,* says the art dealer. If she believes that she should halt the next war then she has to halt that war. The black car! She throws herself in front of that black car. You saw it. That black car was the next war for her. Everybody on earth has the right to halt war.

A ballet starts with a sound. This sound guides the first step. The thin man — he knows it:

She loves dancing. But one has to lead her. But that isn't true. This is not a dance. These are cool exercises and rehearsals. The rehearsal? Perhaps. After all: he knows. That is essential. Somebody who knows the truth about her—and the possibilities—everything. He gives the sign for the first step. With a thin stick. Ping. Against glass or metal. *PING.* That's enough.

The next thing the doctor from Essen says: *She wants to change her life at all costs. But look at all the loony-bins—men and women—thousands of them—they all came in on clouds. It is certainly nice for them to be mad. But afterwards? Then comes the breakdown. Now she flies, everything goes well. Her misfortune starts with the remission. No more poetry.*

I know the loony-bins, the thin man thinks. But when you can't stand normal life anymore you choose the other side. If she understands, the spell will be broken. If she understands love, love will vanish. If there are no questions — then what's left for her? Questions without answers, that's what she needs. She is fed up with solutions.

Look at her, the doctor from Essen says. *She wants to leave the airplane in the middle of the flight. She wants to return down there, to her habits, to 'social security'. Keep seated, Madame,* says the steward-book dealer. The black airplane with its small white circle ascends into the sky as the other plane lands in Berlin. With tears in her eyes she raises her hand: good-bye. *Look down to your feet — go,* says the thin man, pale in his own country. *Go! I will take care of you.*

Where did it start? A long, long time ago. It started at the age of 6. It started when she thought for the first time about the word LOVE. LOVE. That's an unidentified man. The thin man. The white man. The blue-eyed man. The man who talks lit-tle. When he talks, he talks softly. The man in the armchair in front of the white house. The man who doesn't touch her. The man whose name is LOVE. And she married him at age 6. The thinking man. The man who is here—every-where—since always. The picture of love. There it starts. That's for sure.

1970 (E for Easter.) for professor LACAN, U.Z. crazed by happiness since C.R. will buy 5000 tons of opium to destroy H.B. (oh sweatheart).

translation by Frank Mecklenburg

Ali Baba's Cave

Françoise Gründ

Between 1976 and 1981, a new Word appeared within the small world of the performing arts: the *third theatre.* This generic name, promulgated for the most part by the energetic Eugenio Barba, designates—more than this or that direction of research—a state of despair among occidental dramatists. Indeed, the preceding decade (1960–1970) seems brilliant by comparison. But wait; was it really so fruitful? Or is it some trick of memory that retrospectively magnifies the shocks received by the public? These shocks, exaggerated or not, are now part of the the the theatre's historical reality: Ronconi's *Orlando Furioso,* Bob Wilson's *Regard du Sourd,* the relentless investigations of Peter Brooks, Lucinda Childs, Grotowski, Lavelli's frozen operatics, the fulminations of Victor Garcia and the mutant creations of Peter Stein and Giorgio Strehler. All occidental in spirit and formation, these dra-matists stretched the space of theatrical action to include music, singing, dance, gesture, masks, puppets, elocutionary play. What propelled each of them, almost simultaneously, to search for this *other* material, and what was their goal? At the same time that intel-lectuals not specialising in the the-atre at last discovered the explos-ive throat of Antonin Artaud, a hybrid public was descending into Ali Baba's cave, the Theatre des Nations, instinctively—no theory applied—and with disordered, even boiling astonishment. Aware that third-world performances were answering to appetites which they themselves could barely *find,* let alone state, this public greedily ingested the Peking Opera, the Kings of Dahomey, the dancer-stilters of Mali, all on the stage of the Sarah Bernhardt Theatre in Paris. Aware of the distance of their own cosmogony and of their declining sensuality, they were eager to find a fresh mode of com-municating with other peoples of the world, becoming conscious of otherness beyond all strategic and economic consideration. Not that Ronconi, Wilson, Brooks et. al. are simply reflex products of the Theatre des Nations — but their public detection and eventual success did stem from a highly favorable set of circumstances, namely a hunger for difference lingering on the occidental palate.

Over the past ten years, western performance has experienced a profound famine; the public in Europe and the United States has remained more or less permanently unsatisfied. Meanwhile, the cultures of the "undeveloped" world have continued to pursue their own path through traditional means of expression: rituals, music, dance, theatre, often mingled together within one single, total performance. No matter whether these expressions are sacred or profane in *theme*: they are always in-escapably and unshakably related to both the rhythms of everyday life and to the deep consciousness of a Beyond. The guiding mentalities of India, Japan, Afganistan, Korea, Egypt, Mali, Bolivia and Peru (the list could go on) are all tied to strong cosmogonies that no *one* can remember, but that are established for all, and forever, crystallizing within their integral contradictions all the conflictual combinations that might occur in life itself. Patterns of reflection and action for wars, treason, cowardice, aggression, revenge are already set in the marvelously eternal repetitions of the Gods;

mortals have only to invent the forms. Mongolian diaphonics and tongue rolling, the ritual stilt dances of the Makonde in Tanzania, the intricate gestural language of the Kathakali in India and whirling dervishes of Turkey, however exotic they may appear to Western eyes and ears, are never intended to surprise or provoke crisis. The shock that occurs is desired and expected, known in all its details, each expression reenacting what everyone already knows. Consequently, actors and public are released from the weight of history, becoming themselves part of a continuous spatio-temporal gravitation.

Occidental expression, on the other hand, has an *origin,* is *rooted* to a very specific time and space, the Promethean moment. The whole notion of Occidental performance centers around the Promethean rupture of Man from the Universe. It is the moment of the rupture, rather than a deep cosmogony, which is reenacted in occidental performance. In order for this rupture to be concretized within an individual *piece,* an important element must intervene, the element of surprise. The whole western theatre is based on the sudden discovery of the unknown, the "taking" of the spectator by surprise. The western artist and dramatist must be a master of the surprise, must be a perpetual innovator, a novel-ist. This contrasts sharply to the whirling dervish, whose artistry rests assuredly in the interpretative quality of repetition. The western dramatist is obliged to celebrate an individual revolt, to measure swords with the Gods, to separate, to *go off.* Such Promethean drives, running through virtually all western movements in the performing arts, can only lead into a dead end. And those who manage, (at least for a *spell*), to avoid the deadliness of perpetual novelty, do so by way of a trick, a device, an exquisitely refined lie. Or, possibly, they effect a trans-ferral from the image of the Gods to the image of Power (political theatre), depict visions from the past or the future, play with the emotional capacities of the spec-tator, or multiply apparent differ-ences among forms of expression so as to appear all the more mas-terful in putting Humpty Dumpty together again.

It is a commonplace that the occidental has lost its defini-tion of God. The occidental dramatist, in a heroic search for the exercise of this not-knowing, not-knowing put on parade, is suddenly left with empty hands. The elations of rupture and the element of surprise have worn threadbare; there is nothing surprising anymore. Consequently, the Western dramatist begs, borrows or steals. As far as this is concerned, one cannot really blame Eugenio Barba or Peter Brooks. The first takes from the Shamanistic rituals of Venezuela (*The Book of Dances*), from Indian dance (*Marco Polo*), from Peruvian Music (*Come and the day will be ours*). The second attempts to circumscribe a universal man and borrows heavily from the Soufi ceremonies of Iran and Afganistan. Both borrowings are subtle and effective, but regardless of the integrity of the attempt, such rummaging among the collected designations of Otherness may turn Ali Baba's magical cave into a manufactury of white bones.

Where is, then, the answer nowadays? After all the exotic expeditions of the *third theatre,* how, and for what, might occidental performance — if freed from its Promethean pretensions — *come home?*

translation by Brigitte Ouvry-Vial

56

Isla Negra

Ariel Dorfman

If Pablo Neruda had not been a poet, he once declared, he would have built houses. He might have added that, in fact, he *did* build houses. Before he died on September 22, 1973, exactly twelve days after the death of the democratic Chile that he loved so dearly, he had managed to buy three unfinished houses in three different locations, and had spent years enlarging them, appending spires and rooms, galleries and watchtowers, guest houses and libraries.

His third house was his most famous: his home in Isla Negra, a tiny coastal hamlet of rocks, surf, and gulls sixty miles west of Santiago. It too was invaded by soldiers, but not ravaged. This oversight may have been due to the fact that the poet was not in Santiago but there, dying of cancer, when Pinochet's men came. They were looking for weapons, for guerillas, for communists: they opened each book,  original editions of Whitman and Rimbaud; they clicked their flash- lights into his unique collection of shells and of frigates in bottles; they looked behind his 17th cen- tury maps of America and behind the schooner figureheads that he carried back with him from all the corners of the earth; they even searched a small many-colored locomotive in his front yard for the children who came to visit. When the major in charge of the operation confronted the poet who lay in bed, he was flustered, and excused himself. *I'm sorry, sir, but we have been informed that there is something dangerous here.*

During the years of forced exile I had, of course, been unable to visit Neruda's house. One of my first acts once I was allowed to return this September was to visit Isla Negra. If Chile were democratic, it would have been natural not only that I should have gone, but that I would have also slept and worked there. Neruda had left his house to Chile's poets. He had made the Chilean Communist Party, of which he was a prominent member, the executor of that clause in the will. When the junta confiscated all the possessions of left-wing parties, Neruda's magic house unexpectedly fell into their hands. Just as the army major had been taken aback by the actual sight of Neruda, so the government had not known exactly what to do with his house. Even someone as absurd as General Pinochet would have found it beyond the limits of his perverse imagination to solemnly inaugurate Neruda's house and open it to the writers that he has spent ten years persecuting, beating, censoring, and forbidding, removing from jobs and sending into exile. So, the government did the only thing it could do: shut the house up and let it deteriorate. After all, some genius in the police must have thought, how much harm can an abandoned house do?

At first glance it would seem that this prediction is correct. The room where Neruda used to munch cheese and write verse watching the waves burst onto the shore is boarded up. The round-eyed fish he painted on the outer walls along with many other symbols are peeling. One can imagine the books inside growing moldy.

But it is nevertheless a heartening sight. A long fence surrounds the house and on each slat, each vertical board, messages have been scribbled, hundreds, thousands of messages. People have come from all over Chile, and all over the world, to write something on that fence. They speak to Neruda directly, calling him Pablo, and using the familiar *tu* instead of the more distant *usted*. Some are political slogans but most are declarations of love, short poems, random thoughts. At times it is a couple of lovers that sign, lovers that have used Neruda's verses as a bridge between them; very often groups of teenagers; and also whole families. I stopped and was moved particularly by one list of ten people all with the same surname. At the bottom someone had scratched: *And also Pablito (two years old).*

And so, scores of ordinary people had felt that they could not be silent, that their words had enough significance to be left as a gift for others to decipher. By pledging those love letters, by scrawling their names, by thanking a dead man for interceding in heaven and under the earth, by the wild assortment of their grieved valentines, they were telling Neruda how much they missed him, how faraway he was, how near. Some messages were carved into the wood, but most were made with erasible traces of chalk and coal. When the rains came, they washed away those phrases and then others came to write upon the fading words new vows.

Pilgrim's Descent

Maurizio Torrealta

To the Pilgrim nearing its walls, the city appears suddenly ringed by a slimy river, bathed in vapors so dense as to stupify the most travelled vagabonds: barbarians camping at the outskirts, Byzantine astronomers atop floating towers, Phoenician seamen coming from the docks, errant knights in search of adventure, bored squires looking for women, erudite monks just out of the cloister all mingling through the narrow avenues of the capital of all peoples, with no indication of a real coming together.

The Pilgrim essays to grasp the speech of each of these groups, but the seasons allotted to mortal life do not suffice for a clear understanding. Many are the questions raised within the city walls, yet the old narrate that the greater the influx of people, the more vacuous are the answers. Lingering and waiting patiently for the pilgrims at the city gates, the heretics are naturally bent on taking advantage of this situation, ready to draw them into long errisaical promised lands, expecting unlikely catastrophes.

But the Pilgrim knows that what he is looking for is not speech: it is rather the humming of prayers, the chorality of hymns, the mystery of rites that took him in the first place through the narrow avenues of the capital, seeking the mysterious place where speeches are shaped before being pronounced.

He is often comforted in his search by an occasional fellow traveller encountered in the daedalus of alleys by the port, typically in a pub; a scribe who in translating an edict adds on his own the last two commas, or an alchemist who together with the formula of his most poisonous potions furnishes the names of people upon whom to test them.

And it turns out that our Pilgrim meets with Semioticus.

A convent novice too engrossed in the calligraphic revolution of Arabic numbers to be able to participate in the benediction of the Crusades off to the Holy Land, expelled from the convent, Semioticus was too sluggish to explain himself properly and too intelligent to conform, and so he chose the mission of the Prophet.

Who was it that said that speech comes before the hymn, he asserts turning to our Pilgrim, engulfed in alcoholic fumes, *if you follow me to the end you will certainly find speech amidst my scrolls, but the beginning is most assuredly a hymn, a prayer, a choral celebration; it was from a collective rite of dancing people that narration was engendered and ushered forth: follow me to-night and I shall show you the place of origin, the chorus of the satyrs.*

The solitude of the Pilgrim thus finds appeasement, and his search proceeds with the comforting words of the Prophet. For Semioticus cast a long shadow through the fire-filled night, amidst the precipitous irruptions of Mongolian knights, and pointed toward the place of the celebration; and the place appeared after a long and tortuous erring among the shadows.

Under the night sky of Venus, arriving from all corners of the empire, there gather Islamic seamen, scribe monks, Japanese virgins, Arabic jewelers, barbarians long in possession of the truth, all ready to forget for a night the *principio individuazionis,* ready to give themselves the Dyonisiac intoxication of the dance.

Donning the accoutrements of seven different religions, the high priest murmurs strings of meaningless words right in the center of the assembly, while the indistinct mass of people is dancing wildly about.

Stepping hesitantly into the crowd, the Pilgrim is pushed and shoved by the multiform flux of people, then he begins to murmur to himself the first sounds of a prayer, the improvised tune of a thanksgiving song:

Let us reserve for the music-playing priest all the honors typically bestowed upon heads of state, for though his state does not yet exist, nations are often born which never take on the form of a state, like the Assyrians, the Catalonians, the Armenians, the Basques, the Bretons, the Palestinians, the Irish, models of society that become a nation long before they become a state, that become a nation against their becoming a state, people recognizable by their particular way of playing the violin, or wearing a scarf; by the way they stress their r's or step into a dance. May the music live well beyond the night and web the peoples and the races in delicate embroideries; may the unending movement allow the primal mother to become eternally engendering.

Amidst the confounding flux of moving bodies, Semioticus listens attentively to the words murmured by the Pilgrim, then draws him near by tugging at his cloak, and whispers in his ear:

Father Antonin Artaud once wrote, before folly took him: I will believe only in a God who can dance;...and Master Nietzsche wrote: It is by dancing and by singing that man shows himself to be a member of a superior community; he has unlearned how to walk and how to speak and he is about to fly off dancing into the sky;...o my brother, we are witnessing the celebration of a nation of which books know nothing, which explorers have yet to map, yet right here and this very night, upon the ashes of thousands of years of slavery and submission, a nation is coming unto the light, a nation founded on dance. The people about us are not obsessed with the search for a future state, they are not a band of quarrelsome brigands out to protect their territory. Right here and this very night, an ancient rite shall repeat itself, as with the dancers of St. John and St. Vito, the bacchic array of the Greeks, the orgiastic sounds of the Babylonians; man is transformed from artist into a work of art, and he becomes a primate, a goat; a metamorphosis accompanied by the enchanted sound of the lyre, birth before lyric poetry... the moment of the origin of speech.

The throng begins grotesque movements, heads lose their stiffness and dangle undulating and sinuous, shoulders are raised and lowered alternatively and, suddenly, a goatish shape leaps down the stairs and begins to rotate in whirls, the head rather than its feet right in the middle of the feast, the high priest continuing to observe impassively a blank spot in darkness lost.

The Pilgrim responds:

Your words enlighten me, your prophecies reassure me, but your solitude frightens me. You perceive in the present the signs of the future, for you the present is such only as an enunciation of its becoming, you are not participating in the dance, you observe, scrutinize and preach. The high priest instead celebrates the present in its immensity, in its immanence; we are beasts and we are angels, we are the infinite sum of all possibilities. To you, Prophet, what exists is only the ineluctability of becoming, the necessity of having to be, whereas for the high priest what exists is the infinite sum of all possibilities, and you both have cast your glance on the essence of things, and both have tasted the nausea of the existent. But though alone, you have chosen the doctrine of change, you search still for action. In the high priest's celebration, instead, within his painfully veiled glance there is lodged the ultimate attempt for knowledge, the attempt to forget oneself, the attempt to reach the phatic murmur of prayers at the ultimate level of oblivion.

There is an ancient sorrow buried within each race that predates words and speeches and which only the dance can account for: an ultimate attempt to abolish differences and to reestablish possibility. May the prairies of desire be conquered by this nation of dancing satyrs, may the frontiers of the sky of electronic communication become the proper continent for the revenge of the offsprings of the slaves. For years the God Apollo dictated the measure of beauty and the relationships of perfection through the distances and in encounters; for years still the Dionysiac force was compressed by a crooked model and disturbed by the Apollinean parody of beauty, they called it a new wave but it was rather a new wave of old rubbish, a nighttime nightmare of a never lived day. The mysteries of Dionysus have now unleashed the tribality of instincts, the collective rites multiply spontaneously through towns, vales and cities, a new nation is born: it will be years before it shall be baptized and years still until it shall be recognized, equipped with words, outfitted with speeches. . . but the Dionysiac season has begun.

The words of the Pilgrim conquer the nearby, tattered multitude, the feast breaks up in hundreds of tiny groups and at the very center people speak and dance indifferently, and words bear the rhythm of dance and dance the power of words, and chiasmus anagram anacoluthon allusion anastrophe all are realized in the dance as in speech. Semioticus, who during the Pilgrim's speech had listened in wonderment, who had been sensitive to his arguments and the attention that was developing amidst people awaiting to be a sort of public, Semioticus now speaks:

Holy are your words, o Pilgrim. Yes, it is true, the destiny of the Prophet is dying a solitary death without tasting the pleasures of the dance. But perhaps it is owed to precisely this condition that I, able to prophetize what will happen generations hence, choose instead to foresee what will take place in a few days, in a few hours, as I attempt to lose myself in the waves of my frock at every stride, when the satyrs will be able to prophetize and the prophets to dance: then will the throngs move in continuous celebrating migration and the force of history unveil its origin, for this is one of Dyonisius' mysteries. Observe, the nation has a leader, but a leader who speaks not: the leader is a disc jockey, he who speaks by remaining silent, he who knows but repeats with slight anticipation of what people want to hear. All possible speeches have already been made, all possible music has already been composed: to steal the rhythm, the sentence appropriate to that precise instant and to repeat them by bouncing them from one turntable to another for a second only, for the second needed: for truth doesn't exist and this is the only form of knowledge: to know like a scribe, to know like a disc jockey, an act which is possible in any field of enquiry, living in the forgetfullness of knowledge retracing those unique fragments that can be invested with meaning, and using them, repeatedly, obsessively. . . the celestial eye of the satellites has drawn new maps, new frontiers overlay and cover up old ones, new worlds are about to come forth within the old and over the old, new countries extend over the magic waves of the new channels of communication and are waiting only for proper rites to be celebrated; what we see: the races, the hordes, the caravans are not part of an old world, minorities of the peripheric regions of the empire that vindicate a national autonomy, they

61

are not even **gens** *that accept* **gently** *to be part of the empire; what you and I see, Pilgrim, is the* *fourth world.*

And the ceremony slows down, indulging; it wants not to stop, not to act though aware of the moment of its own concluding.

The new nation is born out of these miseries and these sorrows, from these aspirations and this wisdom, from these mysteries and secrets. Mysterious sects are working in the shadows writing new alphabets, new letters and new signs will mark out the peoples, and above all the music, like the drums of the Zulu nation, will call again from valley to valley and from street to street the newly matured races for the new nation.

The ceremony has always a beginning but no end, for in its course something is produced. The very same participants are altered, a miracle takes place and by singing senseless rhymes till obsession — like an affabulaton, like verses from the Koran, like a rosary of Hail Marys — nothingness takes back once again what properly belongs to it, the mystery remaining locked in its necessity and which — thank God! — nobody will understand, not even in front of the evidence.

The pale light of dawn sweetens the night's blue hue, Byzantium is awakened by the cries of the pepper vendor, by the howling of the helmsmen that dock at the piers, by the pawning of imperial cavalries. Nobody realized what was going on.

translated by Peter Caravetta

OZYMANDIAS

Paul Foss

Maps and Images   Maps always accompany movements. Whenever maps are made there have been flows of goods, people, machines, messages. . . War campaigns follow along the lines laid down by maps. So do voyages of discovery, of trade, of colonisation, of scientific enquiry, etc. Even information only flows along routes made possible or designed by maps (telegraph lines, roads and postal networks, media waves, geodetic or intelligence satellites).

But this is not at all to say that any movement must precede its map. When Alexander marches to Pattela, his very course, and what he saw along the way, was directed by the myopia of Hellenic geography with respect to the imagined size of Asia; for instance, despite actual observation to the contrary, he saw the Caspian Sea as a gulf in accordance with the beliefs of the time, as a northeast passage to the Orient. Nothing had changed with the Elizabethans who, much later on, still sought this passage in vain on Alexander's authority, or at least Pliny's. In this case, as in so many others, it is sight which follows the image. In fact, it is possible that flows always follow maps, and never the reverse.

How do maps generate movements, and not the reverse? This might immediately appear to be only a problem which springs from false information. After all, it could be argued that nobody could travel to the east coast of Australia while they did not know where it was, the flow of the first colonists proceeding from Cook's original traversal along it with its consequent mapping. But to reason like this only evades the core of the problem. For we might as well ask why in fact did Cook go precisely in the direction he did or what effect did earlier maps, however "incorrect", of the Great South Land have upon his journey westward from Tahiti. As with all attempts to fix, reduce the pay of referentials, you enter into the maze of infinite regress. The map of Cook folds back on those of William Jansz and Torres, they in turn on that of Magellan and other circumnavigators, eventually to blur in the distance of Marco Polo's narrative "map" or Plato's mythic vision. Or is it a matter of accident? The event defining itself out of the tangled fabric of history?

But looking back into the haze from the portals of prehistory, the vision remains stubbornly clear: an imagining of geographical "otherness," silent conjectures or movements of the mind which experiment with the extent of reality, groping always outwards, a proliferation of images in the order of perceptual spaces. Beyond the horizons of all cartographies, beyond even the image of the "true" nature and constitution of the earth itself, there still remains the activity of image-making for the purposes of experimenting with the real. Map-making is image-making. It is a pure performance, and in that sense, it is always creative of itself. Which is why maps are projections in space of strategies or manoeuvres to come.

The geography of maps is first and foremost that of strategy, not of the earth. And what they refer to or give bearing to is not territory as fixed substance, but territory as fluid field. Hence maps change as do their range of application of Ptolemy. Mercator as well as modern geodetic projections are all equally real, they are all perspectives on real historical movements. Maps neither reflect absolute limits imposed by the earth, nor the serendipity of the eventual. They are equally determinate and imaginary.

It is true that maps concern representation. However, no ideal coextensivity ever exists between map and territory, nor can there be. It is in the difference between the two that the power of maps resides. But the nature of that difference can change. Even when read as simple reflection maps are in danger of making new regions apparent: see the complaints of the English in the sixteenth century concerning the difficulty in obtaining charts of discovery from the East India Companies of Holland and Portugal. By the same token, maps may pervert the reality which underlies them, as with the case of the cartographical delusions of both the Spanish and the Portuguese about which side of the meridian of Pope Alexander VI their respective acquisitions lay. This process of abstraction in maps can deepen so as to mask the absence of any real geographical knowledge; seen, at work for instance, in the maps of Jean Rotz and Desceliers, behind whose juxtaposition of a *Java the Little* and a fantasmic *Java the Great* (the latter extending deep into the Southern Ocean and bristling with familiar names and marks of apparent first-hand observation), was concealed—perhaps for the comfort of the Dauphin to whom they were presented—the embarassing absence of any French presence in that part of the world. Or, finally, maps may be an empty simulation, as in the most beautiful imaginings of Plato about Atlantis or of Marco Polo about mythical Lucach or Beach; which, even if they were not meant as reality, certainly had the effect of sending countless men in search of new lands over the ages and contributed to the way in which they were shaped.

In the second instance, maps are strategems for the abolition of distance. In this function maps rejoin with the true role of visual images. They constitute vanishing lines, escape machines, a beacon of fascination. Look at Gerritsz's map of Dutch contracts with New Holland up to 1628, all those tracings of national prestige remapped on the other side of the globe. Naming and mapping a place is a way to mobolize the pull between "here" and "there." It can set flows going, or freeze them when necessary. But the right image can reduce the effect of distance to locate a place as possible, as within reach, as proximate, by a play of immediacy which changes outland into environment, the hostile into home.

In a way, discovery marks the end of Antipodes as perspective or illusion of space, and the beginning of its transition into the era of geo-strategy or strategies of real space. 1770 is the turning point when Antipodes itself begins to be neutralised. *Space becomes the vista of an all out absorption.* First in the north and the west, then in the east, and finally along the southern coast, image hardens into reality: it is drawn on the map, no longer entirely as an imaginary figure or size, but more and more in place names, in the muddle of tongues, in toponymic lacunae, in accompanying fragments and reports, in travelogues, even on the bodies of the dark and elusive aboriginals. Ultimately, in the great desolate silent nothingness lying just beyond range of sight. At heart still a simulacrum, but bound by a tactical surface of accelerating flows, by the circumference of denial. This is a strategy which has profoundly dominated the course of recent events in Australia. Henceforth, everything will flow into fill the vacuum: goods, people, skills, ideas, military and national presences, etc. Even its own inhabitants, never ever properly naturalised, find themselves having to leave first in order to return as valuable. And any value they have at all involves and dissipates in concentric circles towards the interior: more and more we retire *to the outer rim as if ready to depart.*

It is no longer we who act as balance or sponge for the artefacts of a European civilisation. Everything is sucked into the artefacts of a European civilisation. Everything is sucked into the void to be re-emited back through the stratosphere to help map the territories of the rest of the globe. Like messages skirting in over the horizon. But it doesn't stop there. As we unknowingly aid global surveillance for the Americans, we are in turn spied on. But only because we do not care what goes on in the centre; it is still nothing to us, and can effect nothing. It is a new twist or resurrection of the antipodal simulacrum. In the long run, has anything changed during the millenia: born in the void of space, we are disappearing into it all over again.

OZYMANDIAS   All along the coastline come the sounds of evensong. And everywhere people are waiting. Like those great Easter Island statues, huddled together in the stillness and gazing motionlessly out to sea. Yet nothing ever appears on the horizon to relieve their eternal vigil. Nothing ever returns, everywhere there is only darkening silence. The silence of a nature always alien, that which is endured as one would under life sentence, with the desolation of it carved deep into one's face. It is the bleak and emotionless look of an exile without end. An appeal which has gone unheeded so long that the memory has no words to say it any more. One simply senses it, it hangs in the air. Only just the murmur of lifeless things to count the passing of time.

This is a land without any history. A place which has never truly been inhabited. Its heart has been torn out of the ground and dragged to its furtherest edge. For the purpose of seducing somehaps actual, in the form of magic incantations, sculpted signals or megalithic beacons beaming a message far out into the void. Distress calls, frozen sirens. For the return of a culture long since departed (or which may never have been there in the first place). For the return of the gods.

But the unremitting ocean continues to ebb and flow against its shores, occasionally to throw up driftwood or to wash away loose pieces of the land. But its shores are a barrier. For it is a land completely surrounded by water, an island, an isolate. Even with the island called *continent* the error of isolation merely grows in proportion to the size of its innerspace.

Big or little, islands die from inside out. That is their logic, their common destiny; they only differ in the time it takes. Islands only survive by facing their interior. Until they have either consumed themselves or leaped across great distances to feed on others. Or else sometimes this process does not even start, being petrified in the moment of its birth. Hence the defining property of the insular: the triangular relationship between isolation, interiority and implosion. Though the worst, the minimal term is the one of Easter Islands. Whatever happened there is permanently frozen into a mute ritual of desertion. It is a fractured island, with a massive ravaging of its interior for the sake of great idols erected in the name and in the shape of other deities, then smashed and left to crumble and topple into the sands. That is all that remains of it: a few splintered fragments, holes here and there, indecipherable glyphs, and those huge empty eyes staring blankly out to sea.

Northwest Passage

Michel Serres

The Northwest passage allows the Atlantic and Pacific oceans to communicate within the frigid environs of the Grand Canadian North. It opens and closes, twists itself throughout the huge archipelago along an incredibly complex daedalus of golfs and channels, pools and sounds, between Baffin and Banks. Aleatory distribution and strong regular constraints, disorder and laws. You enter through the Davis Sound, ending in the Beaufort Sea. From there, run over northern Alaska towards the Aleutians, Deliverance, you end up on the name of peace.

For thirty years, I have been navigating among these waters. They are almost deserted, forgotten, as if forbidden. Two cultures are juxtaposed, two families, two collectivities speaking two different tongues. Those who have received a scientific formation have ever since childhood a tendency to exclude from their 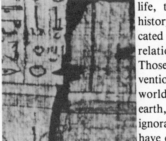 life, their thought, their everyday actions anything resembling history or art, works of language, works of time. Being educated but uncultivated, they are trained to forget humans, their relationships, their sufferings, trained to forget mortality. Those formed by letters are in turn thrown into what one conventionally calls the Human Sciences, where they lose the natural world forever: works without trees or sea, without clouds nor earth, except in dreams or dictionaries. Being cultivated but ignorant, they devote themselves to pointless squabble. All they have ever known takes the shape of bets, fetishes or goods. I fear these two groups may be contesting for belongings that have long ago been carried away by a third group; parasites, uncultivated and ignorant, this third group ordinates and administers the others, enjoying their division, nourishing their split.

I have been very lucky to remain alone for thirty years, working in the passage amidst indifference and silence. I stand in the empty intersection between the two groups, whose cartography I try to narrate. I am not sure to be at the outlet. The passage is rarified and narrow. From the human to the exact sciences, or vice versa, the path does not lead through homogenous, open space. The metaphor of this extraordinarily complex archipelago designated within the Grand Canadian North is exact. Most of the time, the passage is closed, either by lands or by ice, or also because one does get lost.

One usually simplifies by means of a forced choice: continued or discontinued, analysis or synthesis, God or the Devil, yes or no, with me or against me, from two things only one. Yet complexity signals itself in reality, while philosophical dualism calls for a final battle in which new thought dies and the object disappears. The misfortune comes from a simplification by arms. It is this social artifact that one must destroy if one wants to think. The other prejudices are weightless compared to this monstrous animal, stupidity. Yes, struggle is our first habit; it annihilates our intellectual awakening. Yes, thought has no other obstacle than hatred. The misfortune of thought always comes from thought itself.

Translation by Brigitte Ouvry-Vial

The Fourth Dimension

Wole Soyinka

Yoruba myth is a recurrent exercise in the experience of disintegration, and this is significant for the seeming distancing of will among a people whose mores, culture and metaphysics are based on apparent resignation and acceptance but which are, experienced in depth, a statement of man's penetrating insight into the final solution of things and the constant evidence of harmony. The unblemished god, Obatala, is the serene womb of chthonic reflections (or memory), a passive strength awaiting and celebrating each act of vicarious restoration of his primordial being. His beauty is enigmatic, expressive only of the resolution of plastic healing through the wisdom of acceptance. Obatala's patient suffering is the well-known aesthetics of the saint.

For the Yoruba, the gods are the final measure of eternity, as humans are of earthly transience. To think, because of this, 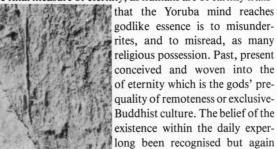 that the Yoruba mind reaches intuitively towards absorption in godlike essence is to misunderstand the principle of religious rites, and to misread, as many have done, the significance of religious possession. Past, present and future being so pertinently conceived and woven into the Yoruba world view, the element of eternity which is the gods' prerogative does not have the same quality of remoteness or exclusiveness which it has in Christian or Buddhist culture. The belief of the Yoruba in the contemporaneous existence within the daily experience of these aspects of time has long been recognised but again misinterpreted. It is no abstraction. The Yoruba is not, like European man, concerned with the purely conceptual aspects of time; they are too concretely realised in his own life, religion, sensitivity, to be mere tags for explaining the metaphysical order of his world. If we may put the same thing in fleshed-out cognitions, life, present life, contains within it manifestations of the ancestral, the living and the unborn. All are vitally within the intimations and effectiveness of life, beyond mere abstract conceptualisation.

And yet the Yoruba does not for that reason fail to distinguish between himself and the deities, between himself and the ancestors, between the unborn and his reality, or discard his awareness of the essential gulf that lies between one area of existence and another. This gulf is what must be constantly diminished by the sacrifices, the rituals, the ceremonies of appeasement to those cosmic powers which lie guardian to the gulf. Spiritually, the primordial disquiet of the Yoruba psyche may be expressed as the existence in collective memory of a primal severance in transitional ether, whose first effective defiance is symbolised in the myth of the gods' descent to earth and the battle with immense chaotic growth which had sealed off reunion with man. For they were coming down, not simply to be acknowledged but to be re-united with human essence, to reassume that portion of re-creative transient awareness which the first deity Orisa-nla possessed and expressed through his continuous activation of man images—brief reflections of divine facets —just as man is grieved by a consciousness of the loss of the eternal essence of his being and must indulge in symbolic transactions to recover totality of being.

Tragedy, in Yoruba traditional drama, is the anguish of this severance, the fragmentation of essence from self. Its music is the stricken cry of the blind soul as it flounders in the void and crashes through a deep abyss of a-spirituality and cosmic rejection. Tragic music is an echo from that void; the celebrant speaks, sings and dances in authentic archetypal images from within the abyss. All understand and respond, for it is the language of the world.

It is necessary to emphasise that the gods were coming down to be reunited with man, for this tragedy could not be, the anguish of severance would not attain such tragic proportions, if the gods' position on earth (i.e. in man's conception) was to be one of divine remoteness. This is again testified to by the form of worship, which is marked by camaraderie and irreverence just as departure to ancestorhood is marked by bawdiness in the midst of grief. The anthropomorphic origin of uncountable deities is one more leveller of divine class-consciousness but, finally, it is the innate humanity of the gods themselves, their bond with man through a common animist relation with nature and phenomena. Continuity for the Yoruba operates both through the cyclic concept of time and the animist interfusion of all matter and consciousness.

The deities stand in the same situation to the living as do the ancestors and the unborn, obeying the same laws, suffering the same agonies and uncertainties, employing the same masonic intelligence of rituals for the perilous plunge into the fourth area of experience, the immeasurable gulf of transition. Its dialogue is liturgy, its music takes form from man's uncomprehending immersion in this area of exist-ence, buried wholly from rational recognition. The source of the possessed lyricist, chanting hither-to unknown mythopoeic strains whose antiphonal refrain is, how-ever, instantly caught and thrust with all its terror and awesome-ness into the night by swaying votaries, this source is residual in the numinous area of transition.

The past is not a mystery and although the future (the un-born) is yet unknown, it is not a mystery to the Yoruba but co-existent in present consciousness. Tragic terror exists therefore nei-ther in the evocation of the past nor of the future. The stage of transition is, however, the metaphysical abyss both of god and man, and if we agree that, in the European sense, music is the direct copy or the direct expression of the will, it is only because nothing rescues man (ancestral, living or unborn) from loss of self within this abyss but a titanic resolution of the will whose ritual summons, response, and expression is the strange alien sound to which we give the name of music. On the arena of the living, when man is stripped of excrescences, when disasters and conflicts (the material of drama) have crushed and robbed one of self-consciousness and pretensions, the Yoruba stands in present reality at the spiritual edge of this gulf, with nothing left in physical existence which successfully impresses upon his spiritual or psychic perception. It is at such moments that transitional memory takes over and intimations rack the Yoruba of that intense parallel of progress through the gulf of transition, of the dissolution of self and struggle and triumph over subsumation through the agency of will. It is this experience that the modern tragic dramatist recreates through the medium of physical contemporary action, reflecting emotions of the first active battle of the will through the abyss of dissolution. Ogun is the first actor in the battle.

The drama which stems from this is not the drama of acting man but that of suffering spirit, the drama of Obatala. Yoruba myth syncretizes Obatala, god of purity, god also of creation (but not of creativity!), with the first deity Orisa-nla. And the ritual of Obatala is a play of form, a moving celebration whose nearest equivalent in the European idiom is the Passion play. The drama is all essence: captivity, suffering and redemption. Obatala is symbolically captured, confined and ransomed. At every stage he is the embodiment of the suffering spirit of man, uncomplaining, agonised, full of the redemptive qualities of endurance and martyrdom. The music that accompanies the rites of Obatala is all clear tone and winnowed lyric, or order and harmony, stately and saintly. Significantly, the motif is white for transparency of heart and mind; there is a rejection of mystery; tones of gesture and music combine to banish mystery and terror; the poetry of the song is litanic, the dramatic idiom is the processional or ceremonial. It is a drama in which the values of conflict or the revolutionary spirit are excluded, attesting in their place the adequacy and certainty of a harmonious resolution which belongs in time and human faith. It is antithetical to the tragic challenge of Ogun in man. The profounder aspect of self-recreation, the anguish of the Will, is the portion of original restoration which has been left to the peculiar talents of Ogun.

The weightiest burden of severance is that of each from self, not of godhead from mankind, and the most perilous aspect of the god's journey is that in which the deity must truly undergo the experience of transition. It is a look into the very heart of the phenomena. To fashion a bridge across it was not only Ogun's task but his very nature, and he had first to experience, to surrender his individuation once again to the fragmenting process; to be resorbed within universal Oneness, the Unconscious, the deep black whirlpool of mythopoeic forces, to immerse himself thoroughly within it, understand its nature and yet by the combative value of the will to rescue and re-assemble himself and emerge wiser, powerful from the draught of cosmic secrets, organizing the mystic and the technical forces of earth and cosmos to forge a bridge for his companions to follow.

It is true that to understand, to understand profoundly, is to be unnerved, deprived of the will to act. For is not human reality dwarfed by the awe and wonder, the inevitability of this cosmic gulf? It must be remembered that within this abyss are the activities of birth, death and resorption in phenomena (for the abyss is the transition between the various stages of existence). Life, the paltry reflection of the forces of the matrix, becomes suddenly inadequate, patronising and undignified when the source of creative and destructive energies is glimpsed. Suffering cancels the opaque pleasure of human existence; suffering, the truly overwhelming suffering of Sango, of Lear, of Oedipus, this suffering hones the psyche to a finely self-annihilating perceptiveness and renders further action futile and, above all, lacking in dignity. And what has the struggle of the tragic hero been, after all, but an effort to maintain that innate concept of dignity which impels to action only to that degree in which the hero possesses a true nobility of spirit? At such moments he is close to the acceptance and wisdom of Obatala in which faith is rested, not on the self, but on a universal selfhood to which individual contributions are fundamentally meaningless. It is the faith of *knowing*, the enigmatic wisdom of spiritual serenity. It is this which is often narrowly interpreted as the philosophy of the African. But philosophies are the result of primal growth and formative experience; the oracular wisdom of a race based on and continually acted upon by the collective experience of the past, present and unborn (prognostic) realities, complements the intuitive glimpse and memory of the heart of transitional being.

The Phrygian god and his twin Ogun exercise irresistible fascination. Dionysus' thyrsus is physically and functionally paralleled by the *opa Ogun* borne by the male devotees of Ogun. But the thyrsus of Dionysus is brighter; it is all light and running wine, Ogun's stave is more symbolic of his labours through the night of transition. A long willowy pole, it is topped by a frond-bound lump of ore which strains the pole in wilful curves and keeps it vibrant. The bearers, who can only be men, are compelled to keep the ore-head from toppling over, which keeps them perpetually on the move. Through town and village, up the mountain to the grove of Ogun this dance of the straining phallus-heads pocks the air above men and women revellers who are decked in palm fronds and bear palm branches in their hands. A dog is slaughtered in sacrifice, and the mock-struggle of the head priest and his acolytes for the carcass, during which it is literally torn limb from limb, inevitably brings to mind the dismemberment of Zagreus, son of Zeus. Most significant of all is the brotherhood of the palm and the ivy. The mystery of the wine of palm, bled straight from the tree and potent without further ministration, is a miracle of nature acquiring symbolic significance in the Mysteries of Ogun. For it was instrumental in the tragic error of the god and his sequent Passion. Like Obatala also, gods commit their error after an excess of the potent draught. Ogun was full of wine before his battle at the head of the Ire army. After his dark deed, the wine fog slowly lifted and he was left with nothing but dread truth. Obatala, moulder of men, fell also to the fumes of wine; his craftsman's fingers lost their control and he moulded cripples, albinos, the blind and other deformed. Obatala the eternal penitent therefore forbids wine to his worshippers in or out of his seasonal rites while Ogun, in proud acceptance of the need to create a challenge for the constant exercise of will and control, enjoins the liberal joy of wine. The palm fronds are a symbol of his willful, ecstatic being.

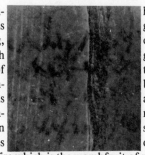

And how else may the inhibiting bonds of man be dissolved when he goes to meet his god, how else may he quickly enter into the god's creative being, or his inner ear and eye respond to the fleeting presences which guard the abode of gods, how else partake in the psychic revelry of the world when it celebrates a crossing of the abyss of non-being? The sculpted rites of the worship of Obatala are rapturous also, but lacking in ecstasy. It is a dance of amelioration to tyrannic powers, not a celebration of the infinite will of the Promethean spirit. The one is withdrawal, the other an explosion of the forces of darkness and joy, explosion of the sun's kernel, an eruption of fire which is the wombfruit of pristine mountains, for no less, no different were the energies within Ogun whose ordering and control through the will brought him safely through the tragic gulf. Even through the medium of this ecstasy, a glimpse is obtained of the vastness of the abyss; the true devotee knows, understands and penetrates the god's anguish. In the centre of the swaying, milling, ecstatic horde where his individuation is routed and he submits to a union of joy, the inner being encounters the precipice. Poised on the heights of the physical mountain-home of Ogun he experiences a yawning gulf within him, a menacing maul of chthonic strength yawning ever wider to annihilate his being; he is saved only by channelling the dark torrent into the plastic light of poetry and dance; not, however, as a reflection or illustration of reality, but as the celebrative aspects of the resolved crisis of his god.

Entropy

Serge Galam

Entropy and disorder Many people of various fields outside of physics have been fascinated by the existential aspect of the second law of thermodynamics. Entropy and its dynamics are thus often perceived only in a conceptual sense, totally cut off from the context of their formulation. By its extension into a realm outside physics, the second law has, in effect, upset all types of people. It would lead us to believe that the world will end ineluctably in a state of total chaos. The more time passes, the more the disorder increases. It is the world's inexorable course towards destruction; life being only a topical fight, intense, but inefficacious, against the spread of decay. The physical law governing the increase of entropy has considerably heightened the pessimist's fatalistic vision of universal history.

Physical meaning of the second law Going to the roots of the second law of thermodynamics one finds that the concern is basically the time evolution of a macroscopic system. In cases of closed systems (i.e., having no exchange with their environment), the equilibrium is reached for the maximum of the entropy, within the external constraints imposed. This means both energetic homogenization as well as maximum spatial disorder.

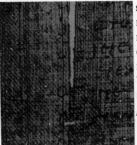

For open systems, *dissipative structures* have been introduced in order to explain local formation of order (living systems) within a general context of increase of disorder. Homogenization means that initial gradients, as for example a gradient in temperature or in concentration, will vanish within a certain interval of time, producing a uniform temperature or a constant concentration throughout the whole system. Levels of energy will also become homogeneous.

In order to achieve a full understanding of the concept of spatial disorder two points have to be clarified. First, entropy is a macroscopic quantity related to the state of a system composed of microscopic elements. Next, entropy concerns the prediction of individual behaviour of elements within the system for any observer situated on a macroscopic level. Maximum spatial disorder means that, for the observer, the probability of finding one element at any given point is the same for all points of available space. This information is therefore not useful since no part of the space can be singled out. The equilibrium of a closed macroscopic system is therefore characterized by an energetic homogenization, and a total accessibility of the available space to each element.

Sociological extension of entropy To understand what these results might mean in a qualitative projection on a sociological level, the equivalences of the basic concepts presented here must first be defined. Homogenization would correspond to an equalization among the members of the society, in other words, a disappearance of social differences. This does not mean that the natural inherent differences between these individuals would vanish, but that many of their socio-economic dissimilarities would. For example, one could associate the wealth of each individual with the level of energetic excitation of each particle. The intrinsic nature of each individual would therefore be explained in a physical analogy by the energetic ground state of the particle. Energetic homogenization leads to a uniformity of the energetic levels of excitation of the particles with no modification of their ground states. Socially, this would mean that each person would have the same economic level without implying uniformity of one's basic nature.

High entropy society or generalized individual nomadism   The qualitative construction of a thermodynamic paradigm of society should, through its results, induce a natural evolution of mankind towards a generalized individual nomadism. In essence, a society entrusted to its own development should attain an ideal state of stability characterized by maximum individual prosperity as well as minimum collective exploitation in an egalitarian economic context. Each individual would receive, according to his needs, whatever necessary to attain the general socio-economic level (energetic homogenization). All available space would be accessible to each person, subject to the same conditions for all. This would mean that travel costs would be fixed regardless of the distance, with the necessary possibility of living at any location for the same price (maximum spatial disorder). The system of State Control would be reduced to a minimum. There would be no information concerning each individual's residence.

Low entropy society or generalized individual sedentarity   Take the inverse of the preceding description: a society with low entropy will be synonymous with a static and totalitarian society. The differences between individuals will be significant, the freedom of movement will be grossly limited, each person will be assigned to move only within strict boundaries, and the State will be assigned to move only within strict boundaries, and the State will have maximum information on each person. The army as a particularistic society represents an example of a sociological structure of very low entropy. A low entropy society thus induces a generalized individual sedentarity.

Collective sedentarity versus individual nomadism   The classical view about nomadism is concerned about the migration of a given society as a whole. We found that the application of the second law of thermodynamics to a society leads to predict the existence of a natural evolution toward total accessibilty for any individual to any part of the internal space of this society. This very fact had been perceived in a negative way as increasing disorder. But by introducing the concept of individual nomadism we obtain a positive view. We are no longer concerned with the collective level of the society but with its individual level. When the society reaches its maximum capacity of collective sedentarity by occupying the whole space available to this same society, a new level of generalized nomadism emerges: *Individual Nomadism.*

74

War of the Worlds

Marco J. Jacquemet

Let us leave to the others the task of describing these two worlds, the first technologically asyntotic and the third precipitately cyclical, in order to deal straight away with their battleground: a no man's land where inevitably these two worlds must meet, or rather conflict. This territory is Time, or better yet, the *notion* of time. And as two tribes following a lion in the same tracks cannot but encounter each other, likewise these two worlds *clash,* anticipating an accelerating pathologic, confused and irresolute behavior. In short, creating a general malaise. Nevertheless, it is still possible to recover two readings: two paradigms of the perception of the time that these two worlds have always utilized in their interpretation of the real. A technological paradigm: historic, evolutionistic and global in the confident linearity of capital; and a magical paradigm: human, agreed upon as individual scansion, cyclical and 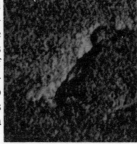 local in the life/death rhythmicity of the nomad tribe. The two readings annul each other and the possibilities of synthesis take refuge in the niche of the imponderable as the capacity to project sinks more and more into the Symbolic, the Magical. The very notion of *model* becomes an anticipation of the future, the future comportment of the world. Magic and technology are falling in step together, if ever they were separated, and yet again their unity is structured around the same temporal anxiety: the search for a prevision that would control the future and erase the past.

The second principle of thermodynamics tells us that every system runs inevitably toward its own disorder inside an irreversible time, that things *do* have an end. And the results that this growth produces inside the Imaginary are devastating. We are at the commission of death as we are conscious of the irreversibility of time.

And the alcoholic, the addict are still the most classic figures of this cultural clash between worlds. Living in the great metropolises they have abandoned a cyclic time but have not succeeded in finding themselves in the progressive rhythm of capital and the instant becomes their only perceivable reality, the world broken up into an absolute discontinuity perhaps never to reform again.

As the social implications of this road to disorder cannot be ignored, society realizes its destiny as that of the lemming and puts on the brakes. The new utopia is *zero growth* permanence of the present. It's awareness of time as a rare resource, indispensable to civilization. And time is running out.

The collective malaise questions itself at an always more rarified time: *zero growth* becomes the warning of a crisis of what is to happen. The 18th century equation future = progress, yesterday's byword, is void of signficance, seriously compromising the very existence of this developmental model. In linguistics we've seen the disappearance of the future. That is, how the old philosophical metaphors of time like past/present/future have vanished. We are now in the presence of a double articulation of the linguistic structure, an actual world (m_0) and a non-actual world (m_j), a world straight from my utterance and a world with a precedent reference (that which at one time was called *the past.* The future disappears as a temporal position resulting simply from a modal investment of the subject in the moment of his utterance, *I will be a soldier* is rather, *I must be a soldier* or *I want to be a soldier.* And no one mourns the disappearance.

The future no longer exists, the future event is no more, and this is the extraordinary creature of the fourth world. Again, the first to acknowledge the transformation are the economists: paper money exists only in terms of a future function. In fact, *what will happen* is literally injected into the very fabric of the present in the form of paper money. The more than a million tales of finance are also the tales of a growing dependence of the present on the future; of a lengthening of the interval between raw materials and finished products, between production and consumption, between the decision to invest and the actual gain, the allocation of work and the collection of payment.

Credit necessitates the future — the brightest possible. But to this linear and cumulative time of the social structure, we are obliged to set alongside a second time, the time of cyclical crises, time of conjuncture, oscillatory, already inside the concept of the economic cycle.

Pearl waited two months before obtaining permission to open a checking account at the Metropolitan Savings Bank. She was furious and didn't understand why they wouldn't take her money immediately. How in the world was it possible her money had no value? Because if the future no longer exists, her money is worthless. Thus, it would have been much easier for her to open an account if the bank had placed faith in her as an individual rather than regarding her solely as a possible client. And to obtain one's trust in a moment where there is no future is most difficult.

At this point it is necessary to look for a solution that assembles the continuities into some scheme, even if only locally. In this sense one doesn't have to look for an impossible synthesis between these two worlds, rather the research must begin with local continuities in order to find there a rhythm in the global discontinuity of the planet.

Rhythm, being the new parameter of analysis, gathers up the temporal scansion with the idea of linking itself to the concept of computer time as absolute acceleration of the discontinuity, as possible interpretation of the cyclical/progressive dichotomy. In the immediacy of informatic processes it is possible to reconstruct figures that are still sensible *(rhythm creates the form)*, to connect various levels by throwing bridges between these reservoirs of information.

translation by Louise Travetsky

Detention

Ninotchka Rosca

On Sundays, it was open-house at the men's detention centre. Wives, mothers, sisters, and other blood relatives were allowed to come in and stay for four hours. It was the week's big event. When it was cancelled on Red Alert days, half the men went crazy with loneliness

I joined the wives every Sunday and, under armed escort, crossed over to the detention building where Louie waited. Like the others, he had already strung a damp blanket about the lower bunk of his double-deck bed. The ceilingless roof of galvanized iron sheets focused the sun's heat rays down into that hall of three hundred men and their visitors. The blanket, slowly drying, cooled the air about the bunk. It also gave some privacy.

Once, the guards caught a gambler and his wife making love within their improvised tent. Since then, on Sunday after-noons, the loudspeakers blared out commands for the blanket-curtains to be raised. The men complied, but as the hours passed and the heat intensified, the blankets would come down again.

Sometimes old Sammy, who had spent twenty years in prison, joined me and Louie. He told stories about his stay at the old Bilibid. Once he said to me: Do not worry; the first five years are the most difficult, but once that's over...I had been under detention for only four months.

He told us about a show Xavier Cugat and his troupe put up at the old Bilibid. There was a beautiful blonde with Cugat, and the men shouted themselves hoarse cheering her as she cha-cha'd like a worm in heat. When the show was over, about a hundred men lined up against a low hedge to wave good-bye to the blonde as she boarded the bus that had brought her to the prison. She waved back, taking her time and blowing kisses. The men cheered and waved with their left hand. With their right, they were busy masturbating behind the hedges. It was, Sammy said, so sad...

Louie and I weren't sad. We were young and painlessly in love. Nothing, we thought, could touch that — not the barbed wire, the burlap sacks at the window, the rancid starch odor of the soldiers' uniforms. We lay on the bunk, holding each other, our breaths mingling. Sometimes I fell asleep; he would sleep then — both of us cocooned in the breath of that blanket drying in the afternoon. We had each other and that was enough.

Of course, it wasn't. It took months before I understood that. Given freedom once more, I would wake up in the middle of the night and listen. There were sirens in the distance. I would feel Louie breathing, and I knew his eyes were also open in the dark. We would wait for the sirens to approach, shout at the house, and recede again. I told myself over and over again that we lived near a hospital and that they were ambulance sirens. It didn't help. I still woke up.

During the day, everything was normal. Louie went off to his work. I faced the typewriter. Then, suddenly, it would come: a wave of desolation. I would pack my clothes, tripping over suitcases in my hurry, and in the next instant I would be frozen by the thought that there was nowhere to go, nowhere to go at all. I would empty the suitcases, put away my clothes again.   But even in that , there was no sense of home.

from 'The Monsoon Collection,' courtesy of Queensland Press

Vagabondage

Henri Pierre Jeudy

The vagabond is for the city what the virus is for the body. Permanent absence for which the world map and the body map are equally insufficient. The idea is to kill space in order to disperse in it any kind of corporeal representation. Vagabonds are not excluded from the social body as delinquents, but rather serve as scapegoats; being urban sores, they animate the process of a necessary rupture between social bounds and social order. They do not convey a violent threat, but do exhibit the insidious power of a unity distortion. The body of the vagabond, its displacement outside the limits of space, makes the very process of decomposition esthetic, even vital. Vagabondage is tied to oral and viral otherness, to all forms of exchange that modern societies have caused to disappear.

Wandering thoughts, ori-gin without end. World images cast adrift, vagabond eye. Virul-ence has its own rhythm, one through which the figures of unity metamorphysize; thus references and locations are displaced, and social prophylaxy is transgressed. Yet, in the hyper-vaccinated uni-verse of industrialized societies, is it sickness alone that creates other modes of exchange? Is it the simple absence of representation for corporeal integrity that gen-erates the almost magical power of vagabond metaphors? As long as decomposition is not per-ceived as the consequence of jubilation, it continues to sign out death. The system of ruptures, however, the blast of management obsessions, is the only chance the body has to escape its own mortiferous drive for conservation.

The lizard, when one catches its tail, sheds flesh so as to pursue its own way. This practice of autotomia is not far from the practice of vagabondage. The vagabond's body, probably dead, no doubt drowned and wounded, leaves the territory where it might be recognized, pitches life somewhere else, simulates and parodies death as a way of depriving death of the power to end life. In the name of survival, should we too wait till the *last* moment to cut off our tails?

translation by Brigitte Ouvry- Vial

Angel in the Fourth World

Timothy Simone

The pale blue glow of the video screen lights up the face of a man. His name is Angel. Angel is employed as a switcher by the City University's Telematic Recoding Information Project (TRIP). Cross-referencing incoming data fed by the University's transponder stations positioned around the world, Angel retracks the data to the appropriate academic department. As Angel's fingers play compulsively over the keyboard, he is unprepared for the wash of red that spreads across the empty terminal screen. The image needs to be refreshed, thinks Angel by reflex, at a refresh rate of 300Hz. But through reflex he is seized by a disturbing homesickness for a universe that at one time beat like a heart.

From the pile of the day's program modules, Angel selects a card. Inserted in his microprocessor it renders a topo- graphical representation of his connections to 10,000 people beginning with his immediate biological family and spreading outwards. After viewing the spread of these interconnecting relational vectors through pri- mary, secondary, and tertiary stellar zones, he finds, at a peri- pheral position, a person just like him, born the same time as Angel. He had heard of Network Inter- ception Games (NIGS) where the entirety of an individual's social and psychological lineage would be inverted across the spectrum of past and present social linkages in a feedback loop resembling the carrier tunnels used for particle acceleration in boson (z^0) identification experiments. Any operator equipped with a quadrangular disc conversion system could play. In its simplest form NIGS could encapsulate sampled influences from a totality of social and psychological inputs responsible for operator identity formation within a standardized reversible matrix, bounce them off a current link status read-out, and redeploy the in- fluences back across the pathways where such influences had converged upon the operator. Each ac- tivist in the game would, in turn, be confronted as the recipient of signals and influences which he had initially disseminated or re-directed—a position in which the activist would be catapulted to another time dimension in order to preclude self-cancellation. Every player would literally become a piece of each other so that, at any given second, two or more players would recognize themselves as the same, or a single operator's code identification matrix would be altered so as to prevent operator recogni- tion in any given transmission.

The difficulty was that the game entailed such a horizontal spread that volitional participa- tion was often irrelevant; it was impossible to tell when the game was in progress and who was play- ing. The telenet channels over which the game was played were especially vulnerable to renegade pro- grammers who, these days, were piggy-backing all official transmissions, attempting to displace past real egos with simulated versions whose inadequacies tended to deceive the operator with false catas- trophies. In such instances of confusion, the operator would seek arbitration from designated ref- erees. However, since the renegades operated through hit and run interceptions, the lag time between the operator's request for arbitration and the referee's judgement was usually too great for any viable assistance. Once initiated, the game had to continue non-stop since prolonged vacations were only possible through the unanticipated lulls achieved when there was an excess of countervailing gridlocks.

For all the techno-liminoid complexity, the stark reality remained that Angel had been impeded/expanded by a second Angel logging in only under the name Ikabwa (the Fulani name for Angel). There were Fulani all over now. Angel knew that many had access to the enormous transmission systems established for the burgeoning uranium processing plants in the Azoui strip of Northern Chad and that many more were operating freelance from the huge ramshackle two bedroom single story cottages of the inner Los Angeles suburbs. After radically altering the drug business in Europe, many Fulani bought into the Algerian-Lybian brokerage interests catering to workers in the Sahara Development Zones. Although not lacking in the expertise for telenet gaming, the Fulani's historical nomadism made them the top peddlers of adventurism that required actual physical movement, so it was a surprise for Angel to see a Fulani derivative on the scene, the Fulani being famous for profiteering in risk junkets where a person would be relocated within someone else's psychological crisis. The traders would then collect on the postponed dividends of the time commodity shares market. Preliminary Pixel graphic read-outs indicated Ikabwa's current placement as the LA Zone. But, as always, Angel had to make sure these initial read outs were not confounded by his aesthetic preferences. He once had a Japanese girlfriend, Sumiko, who worked as a receptionist at the agro labs in Riverside, a suburb of Los Angeles where many of these Fulani had begun to buy up desert land. Even in times of crisis, Angel was still capable of reverting to key frames of long afternoons staring at the desert through glass enclosures, curling his toes around Sumiko's thick nipples, listening for hours to her stomach. Perhaps captivated by this sweetness, Angel does not notice his terminal's gift of a diagram of Ikabwa's vaginal oscillations on the screen.

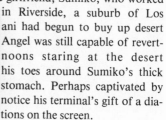

In the miniaturization of civilization, the body is a mobile wound, a synaptic vacancy through which pass alien force fields on their way elsewhere. No longer does the brunt of one's sociality end up at the rim of the cervix. What attracts people now is what is not happening: the reassurance that there is no sex happening, no communication. The operator seeks to defer knowledge to another trick language. People are not looking to enter each other because the entry is already happening outside of anybody's control. The smile is for the camera, the touch is for the memory transducer, the sweat is for the polygraph, and the gaze is for the white cliffs that signal the shore of an operator-response lag.

Angel must get back to the machine. He picks up another card and keys LA. He scans the streets of the eastern most barrios with their "mira-mommy" call-response choruses engaging in some midday dust and crystal trading. It is still within these barrios that any operator can come across an informer lacking sufficient time-credit to get off on the procured supply. There are mostly Japanese and Mexicans out today, not any Fulani, so Angel heads downtown. The terminal offers a variety of "brochures" for the travel. There is the ten minute plan that can take the operator through the Chinatown card games where informants have a 3 pt. rating edge in locating Fulani interceptors and then to the Mexican Soccer League betting parlors for confirmation. Or there is the more risky two minute special that goes right for the Asante and Zulu financial consultants hungry for the "get high" on siesta. Although quick, their veracity is not amenable to any reconfirms in the immediate area. Although he knows that his vulnerability to outside application programs exceeds the effectiveness of the systems assessment monitors he can use, Angel mechanically keys his girlfriend Prise on the monitor. Prise is a demographer who evaluates population deconcentration policies for the Transnational Research Institute for Population Studies (TRIPS) which is a stone's throw from Angel's apartment. He divulges nothing of his predicament to her, aware that his status has always been tentative in her life. Prise, thoroughly adept at synchronizing her emotional capabilities to the technofunkaleptic prescriptions of her time, rarely empathises with crises situations and is accustomed to dismissing them as cognitively shallow procedures for self-revisionism. She prefers the arduous deliberations over outerwear and the attempts to produce maximum kinaesthetic submissions in her listener. While successfully warding off any thoughts of bumping Prise off during afternoon tea, Angel begins to feel pulls toward another submission. Angel checks for deficiencies in his immunization against "breaking." He finds that fear walks on its hind legs as violence puts its wild mouth over legends which defy designation in the circuitry of possible transmissions. The operator is belabored with the specific instructions and the multiple feed into the empire of his self-consciousness. Only once before, having glanced at the video of the immense bread lines in the Ruhr, where hundreds of thousands lined up aside the closed steel mills waiting for rations, did Angel have a taste for the invisible resignations lurking in the smiles of the refuse. There is a compatibility between the capacities of the machines with those illiterate in using them. As the recombinant programs of the microprocessor are able to jump from their silicon harnesses so do the tribes left behind use each opportunity to produce contingent and open-ended results. The

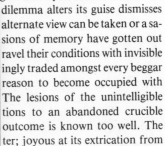

speed at which Angel's current dilemma alters its guise dismisses the slick facility through which an alternate view can be taken or a sasions of memory have gotten out lient curiosity applied. Transfuravel their conditions with invisible of hand. Everywhere minds eningly traded amongst every beggar cortical splicings that are unknowreason to become occupied with and diplomat. There is no good The lesions of the unintelligible keeping the body alive or dead. tions to an abandoned crucible enjoin their momentary satisfacoutcome is known too well. The edited from the code books. The ter; joyous at its extrication from certainty becomes a laughing matendless cycles of deferment, certainty can finally take its place at the table with the wicked and maligned. Those who have been excluded from everything have no reason to get involved in the demise of those who did the excluding. In the lapses of constant control emerges a "middle seeing" where information is gleaned through no reliable procedures and where the blood of the retina mixes with the sebaceous memory of the nomad. Angel reaches for another card and keys the streets once again. Underneath the arched backs of sweet delinquents giving "it" up willingly to prowlers on their way to another fabricated doom, in the whispers of eastern star-crossed lovers who mingle around street corner trash fires, and in the concentrated stares of feral children sneaking away from home on the undersides of tanks deployed to put down some constant third world rebellion, Angel attempts to register Ikabwa. He attempts to locate himself.

Checking with Transmigration Control, Angel discovers that Ikabwa had left LA after having been in prison for one month. She had been picked up for trafficking in internal passports—a petty crime considering the vast array of skills at her disposal. Often times, engaging in such minimal infractions was simply a ploy to gain access to the incarceration centers. The police and other paramilitary control agents constituted an autonomous sector. They trained incarcerated felons in a variety of extortion plots, rub-outs and corporate theft schemes. Upon the prisoner's conditional release, s/he was deployed by the police to carry out numerous pre-conceived jobs. These efforts had been initiated to keep renegade criminals from dominating the subversion trade. To the average escapero on the street, a jail term was a luxury and guarantee for living since the person refused arrest was left to fend for himself, condemned to preying on the crumbs of other escaperos also preying for crumbs. In the Vestige Encampments that circled the urban sectors, full of third world refuse, there was simply not that much to steal. Within these Zonas de Tolerancia, the supply of flesh and dope exceeded the demand, making it difficult to concentrate the trade within structures that would permit more than the petty cash needed to buy intestines and asquinera in the large open-air markets. At times, those who worked for the police would attempt to establish their own clandestine organizations within the encampments. However, the focus of such activity was the production for export since attempts to undercut official prices on the black markets of other sectors were the only means to make cash profits. Such a nexus of trade was, additionally, the only way to ensure a small measure of freedom from police surveillance since there was a great deal of competition amongst the different police organizations in the various sectors for spaces of jurisdiction. The more operatives in the Brooklyn encampments could cooperate with their Jamaican, German, and Nigerian counterparts in the trade of a variety of consumerables, the greater leverage operatives had in instituting their authority in their own sector. Although the police still exerted nominal control, the fluid and constantly revamped associations among the populations of the Vestige Encampments provided some space, however small, for renegade operatives. With the capacity for large scale disruptions of important systemic functions in the hands of albeit exceedingly well-trained and developed cadres, emphasis on the need for large scale popular mobilizations had disappeared from anyone's vernacular. Although no such cadres had surfaced to achieve any discernable effect (separate from actions initiated by the police themselves), the police were, nevertheless, worried that new breeds waiting for the right moment were hidden in the corridors of the densest favelas with the crowds of galinazos and casquilleros. They fret over babies weaned on ancient asiatic modes of psychic weaponry. Under the cloaks of the faceless rellena peddling his little papeletos of dust and crystal is a gamine being readied to take on the world.

If Ikabwa is a known renegade, Angel doesn't like the idea of messing with the cops. But this is a game Angel has no choice but to play. He keys New York Zona Negra Control and discovers that Ikabwa has been moving with an old Trinidadian man named Euclides who shined Malcolm X's shoes back in the days when Black nation building was either a realistic dream or the funniest joke in town. Together they had been circulating through the Vestige Encampments using Ikabwa's university instilled bioengineering skills to unfold an architecture of vanishing points—an effort which, even in the impossibility of secrecy, resisted decoding. Initial read-outs indicated a rudimentary ability, on their part, to make existences disappear from all known methods of person identification. Perhaps the mechanics of their work simulated, in a psychic fashion, the methods of extermination preferred by the futurists currently in power. If the simulation were precise enough, the adjustments required in the surveillance software could not be made without implicating the current methods of control as a threat to that control. Nothing in Ikabwa's university transcripts indicated such sophistication. But in these times of accidental skill acquisitions, it was difficult to adequately evaluate competence levels without a complete holographic analysis of cortical functioning, and such analyses were, themselves, imprecise if dependent upon the subject's mere acquiescence to the procedures entailed. Acquiescence was all that could be certified these days, volition having joined intention as an unquantifiable and, thus, irrelevant commodity.

After reaching Zona Negra control, Angel decides to pursue the hunt alone. He reaches Unit 3 in Brooklyn, what used to be known as Brownsville. There is an urban herb smoke screen over psyche white jack sperm candles lined along the periphery of a vacant lot sowed with yohimbe weeds ten feet tall camouflaging a pit of frying chickens hissing at the encirclement of now silent speakers, portable mixing machines, synthesizers, and generators. A chanting dj lifts an amber-encrusted dagger over a spotted leopard held immobile by women with square haircuts tugging at the animal's bound legs with the thick sinew of their own lacerated thighs. The fight in the beast leads them into a frenzied mimickry of possessed asthmatic lungs as small nappy-named children, clutching gris-gris in their hands, lose their heads in the oversize carved masks strewn through the lot by other tribes on their way to the suburbs. It is a ceremony of picking it, stalking it, sticking it, sucking it, shucking it, faking it, fucking it, going down on it, working it, breaking it. A line of fifty police vehicles wait at a red light down the avenue waiting for the pussy to dry and the chicken to acquire its golden brown hue before it moves to cordon off the lot with bull horns and day-glow night sticks. Blue uniform versus oiled black bodies blue in the acrid haze of ritual fire. As the police move in across the line of candles, switches are flicked and plugs inserted spewing forth a massive amplification of back-beat scrapings in razor sharp lives fucking the shit out of electronic drums snaring orgasms of such high-pitched frequencies that window shields are shattered into the laps of those cops who remained behind the wheel. Under the cover of this invisible shield of deployed sound, Euclides and  Ikabwa slip past the encroaching formation of police and disperse in the direction of more aban-doned buildings which will be torched and then cleared to pro-vide more vacant lots, more wild-erness. Today there is no shortage of wilderness. The ground floors are being cleared away as popu-lations move to the upper stories. Increasing acreages of desertion inhabit the old industrial bases as the tonnage of steel mills is mea-sured in rust instead of chrome bars and welded machinery. Flat cars, once carrying spools of tung-sten chord or bushels of wheat, lie upended on the split tracks of rail-way yards engrossed in the humid persistence of urban flora. The large warehouses, once sheltering inventories of bolts and planks of timber, now amass rodents from the great plains. The stoke holes of the foundries are smutched with the burnt feces of vagabonds rummaging through the stale bread still impeccably wrapped in the lunchpails of the former working classes. An empty water tower shields an eye observant of the rough and tumble rampancy of aspirant warriors setting blaze to heaps of automotive carcasses and bales of yellowed shipping forms in hopes of some pythogenic salvation. Over this urban wilderness criss-cross the vestiges bathed in cobwebs and a gritty dimness: the burdens on the hun-ched shoulders of old Japanese women; the manic thrust of a Puerto Rican glare turning the cor-ner; the full-tooth smile of a Chicano girl seeing the vision of her dead brother in a rainbow pool of water, sludge, and oil and; the skin-jimmying flagrancies of Black anthropologists on sabbatical.

Angel has been trained to always sense something lurking. He has become accustomed to a bone-chilled unease in every understanding, in every appetite for information. Something else rules as a perpetual shadow. Just as wildebeasts clammored over nettled thickets of sagebrush in amphetamine driven chewings of fresh gazelle, the urban vestiges rampage the old enterprise zones hunting fresh gambits.

Ignoring all other obligations, Angel spent days tracking Ikabwa through this wilderness. His administrator from TRIP had interrupted his transmissions several times to reprimand him for his laxity in doing his work and warned of his eventual dismissal if he continued to ignore the requirements of his switching post. The administrator, long sensitive to the demands of such isolated labor and who had, for years, railed against the information sector's disregard for the diminishing social capacities of its operators, counseled Angel to take a brief leave from his machines. Since NIGS was officially shunned, especially during work hours, Angel alluded to problems with his girlfriend. Attributions of operator insufficiency to domestic nausea was a standard means of accounting for deviations inindividual behavior to the apparatchki.It was true that he had been obsessed with Ikabwa, a fascination that extended beyond the interest required by the game player in the subveiter who links herself to all of the player's known identification modules. Angel had spent days observing Ikabwa travel from one incendiary lot to another, rousing the dulled passions of the vestiges with reality-feasting incantations to the margins of regeneration. The tribal effusiveness of the vestiges surprised Angel. He was used to their blood-thirsty craving for moments of temporary unconsciousness which quelled any sustained deliberation on their status or coordinated deployment of their movements. He continued to track Ikabwa through a series of seemingly disconnected and inexplicable acts: spending hours braiding the nappy and greying hairs of elderly women moving the entirety of their possessions from one block to another; crawling along the heat ducts that ran underneath the large housing projects to embroider indecipherable glyphs of red thread on the woolen trousers of the dead that were often tossed there for lack of funeral money; donning the white uniform of a hospital nurse and surreptitiously wetting the anguished eyes of a newborn in a nursery with the sinewy drool of saliva left from a calescent kiss to the forehead and; bathing the sores of a perhaps senile Euclides, whose legs were always wounded during nocturnal stumblings through iron pilings. In the messy residues of these archaic displays of affection, there was something else that Angel could not locate.

Prise had visited Angel several times during the week attempting to entice him away from the game. At other times Angel would have embarrassedly welcomed Prise parading around in a black leather jacket, her body stripped naked below the waist, and would have succumbed to her overtures to ride her quivering mound of spongy tissue around the carpeted basin surrounded by floor to ceiling windows. He would lose himself in the dizziness as he stared at the surrounding buildings tumble in circular rotations as she would spin his body, top to bottom, in the release of her orgasm. But this time, although he wanted any excuse to extricate himself from a fascination quickly assuming the dread of historical determinism, he could not tear himself away from the pile of self-control cards. Angel thought that Prise was performing this intended comfort more for her own narcissistic gratification, linking her womanhood to a war between information and sex, then for a concern with his state of mind. Yet, he had made only feeble attempts to entice her curiosity or provide her some sense of the magnitude of his questioning. Each initial response appeared to chide him for a reawakening surfeit of moral anxiety. Angel felt a certain sadness in how their relationship had been reduced to exhausted erotic adventurism. Although raised to distance herself from the often debilitating emotional tenors of her gender, no longer marketable in the recesses between labor and more labor, Prise had still, in the past, been willing to risk a vulnerability and soothing ingenuousness to their verbal excavations for a shared feeling. It was as if Angel and Prise believed that whatever developed between them could be protected from the reckless groping for personal advantage. Her facile insistence on security was not indigenous to her character. There was simply no context whereby sexual intensity could convert to trust. Angel knew that his capture in Ikabwa would have occurred regardless of the Fulani's gender, but the fact that Ikabwa was a woman provided an unchartable supplement. A supplement. A supplement he was compelled to taste if never understand.

Angel's fingers continued to play compulsively over the keyboard. He is unprepared for the wash of red that spreads abruptly across the terminal screen. The image needs to be refreshed, thinks Angel by reflex, at a refresh rate of 300Hz. Through reflex, he is seized by a disturbing homesickness for a universe that at one time beat like a heart.

An Event in the Body

Lynne Tillman

Dr. Rene Richards, the transsexual tennis player and surgeon who was not allowed to switch in tennis so as to compete as a woman, was interviewed on late night television.

As part of her narrative, Rene Richards explained that when she was still a man she fathered a child, a son. After his operation, sensitive to her son's needs, she acted as both father and mother to him. She made him dinner, but also took him to ball games. She was his pal.

The interviewer, fascinated, leans forward on his chair and asks, *But what does your son call you?* Touching the pearls around her neck, Rene Richards smiles and says, *He calls me Daddy.*

Out of Motown

Cornell West

Motown was the center of Afro-American popular music in the sixties and early seventies —with the phenomenal success of over 75% of its records reaching the top ten Rhythm and Blues Tune Charts in the mid-sixties. The musical genius of Stevie Wonder, Michael Jackson and Lionel Richie; the writing talents of Smokey Robinson, Nicholas Ashford, Valerie Simpson, Norman Whitfield, Barrett Strong, Eddie and Brian Holland, Lamont Dozier and Marvin Gaye; and the captivating performances of The Temptations, The Miracles, The Supremes, The Four Tops, Gladys Knight and The Pips, The Jackson Five and The Commodores set Motown far above any other recording company producing Afro-American popular music.

Motown crossed the color line for the first time. The most successful Motown figures— Diana Ross, Stevie Wonder, 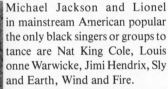 Michael Jackson and Lionel Richie—now have secure status in mainstream American popular music. And outside of Motown, the only black singers or groups to achieve such trans-racial accep- tance are Nat King Cole, Louis Armstrong, Johnny Mathis, Di- onne Warwicke, Jimi Hendrix, Sly and the Family Stone, Lou Rawls and Earth, Wind and Fire.

At its height, Motown produced smooth, syncopated rhythms (like James Brown or The Watts 103rd Street Rhythm Band); restrained call-and-res- ponse forms, not antinomian anti- phonal styles (as with Aretha Franklin or the late Donny Hath- away); and love-centered romantic lyrics, not racially oriented social protest music (like Gil-Scott Heron or Archie Shepp). Yet Motown delicately and wisely remained anchored in the Afro-American spiritual-blues impulse.

There is little doubt that Motown produced some of the great classics in Afro-American and American popular music. The Temptations' *My Girl, Since I Lost My Baby, You're My Every-thing;* The Miracles' *Ooh Baby Baby, Choosey Beggar, Here I Go Again;* Marvin Gaye and Tammi Terrell's *Your Precious Love, If This World Were Mine, Ain't Nothing Like the Real Thing;* Stevie Wonder's *For Once in My Life, My Cherie Amour, You Are The Sunshine of My Life;* and Gladys Knight and the Pips' *Neither One of Us* all stand the test of time.

As Motown became more commercially successful with the larger white American au-dience, it began to lose ground in Afro-America. On two musical fronts—fast funk and mellow soul—Motown faced serious challenge. On the first front, Motown had never surpassed James Brown. Yet Motown had produced music for Afro-America to dance—to twist, jerk, boogaloo, philly dog, and skate. With the appearance of George Clinton's innovative Funkadelic and Parlia-ment, a new wave of funk appeared: technofunk. Never before had black folk heard such delib-erately distorted voices and contrapuntal rhythmic effects filtered through electronic instrumental-ities. Building principally on James Brown, the Funkadelic's *I Wanna Know If It's Good to You, Loose Booty* and *Standing On the Verge of Getting It On* sounded musically revolutionary to the ears of black folk. Motown quickly moved into technofunk with The Temptations' successful *Cloud Nine, I Can't Get Next To You* and *Psychedelic Shack,* but it was clear that the change of image (and personnel) could not give Motown hegemonic status on fast funk.

On the second front—that of mellow soul—Motown had no peer until the rise—precipitated by the roaring success of The Delfonics—of the Philly Sound at Sigma Sound Studio in Philadelphia. The poignant music and lyrics of Kenneth Gamble and Leon Huff, Thom Bell and Linda Creed, Joseph Jefferson, Bruce Hawes and Yvette Davis, Norman Harris and Allan Felder surfaced in the late sixties and early seventies with force and potency, as witnessed by the popular songs sung by The O'Jays, The Spinners, Harold Melvin and The Blue Notes, Blue Magic, Teddy Pendergrass, Major Harris, The Jones Girls, Lou Rawls and even Johnny Mathis. Furthermore, the noteworthy presence of Harlem's The Main Ingredient, Chicago's The Chi-Lites, Detroit's (non-Motown) The Dramatics, Jersey City's The Manhattans and Los Angeles' The Whispers, on this front yielded a more diverse situation.

The early seventies witnessed slightly more political overtones in Afro-American "I'm Black and I'm Proud," popular music. Surprisingly, the political ferment of the late sixties did not invoke memorable musical responses on behalf of popular Afro-American musicians. The youthful black market thrived on music for dance and romance; and such music was the mainstay of the late sixties. As the Vietnam War intensified (with over 22% of its U.S. victims being black), the drug culture spread and black 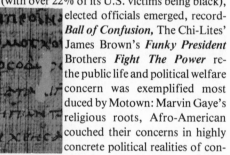 elected officials emerged, recordings such as The Temptations' *Ball of Confusion,* The Chi-Lites' *Give More Power To The People, (people It's Bad)* and The Isley James Brown's *Funky President* Brothers *Fight The Power* revealed more explicit concern with the public life and political welfare of Afro-America. Ironically, this concern was exemplified most clearly in the greatest album produced by Motown: Marvin Gaye's *What's Going On.* True to their religious roots, Afro-American popular musicians and writers couched their concerns in highly moralistic language, devoid of the concrete political realities of conflict and struggle. Marvin Gaye's classical recording openly evoked Christian apocalyptic images and the love ethic of Jesus Christ.

The watershed year in Afro-American popular music in this period is 1975. For the first time in Afro-American history, fast funk music seized center stage from mellow soul music. Given the demand for nonstop dance music in discotheques in the early seventies, and the concomitant decline of slow dancing and need for mellow soul, black dance music became dominant in Afro-American popular music. Barry White's sensual upbeat tunes, Brass Construction's repetitive syncopations, Kook and the Gang's distinctive Jersey funk and Nile Rogers and Bernard Edwards' classy chic are exemplary responses to the disco scene. Yet the most important Afro-American response to this scene occurred in 1975 when George Clinton and William "Bootsy" Collins released two albums: Parliament's *Chocolate City* and *Mothership Connection.*

By building directly upon Clinton's Funkadelic, such as deploying the same musicians, Parliament ushered forth the era of black technofunk—the creative encounter of the Afro-American spiritual-blues impulse with highly sophisticated technological instruments, strategies and effects. Parliament invited its listeners, especially the dwellers of Chocolate cities and to a lesser extent those in the Vanilla suburbs, to enter the Fourth World, the world of black funk and star wars, of black orality, bodily sensuality, technical virtuosity and electronic adroitness. The cover of the first Parliament album, *Chocolate City,* portrayed Washington, D.C.'s Lincoln

Memorial, Washington Memorial, Capitol Building and White House melting presumably under the heat of black technofunk and the increasing *chocolate* character of the nation's capital. The album contained only one mellow soul song (*I Misjudged You*) a mere ritualistic gesture to the mellow pole of Afro-American popular music. The second album, *Mothership Connection*—now joined with the leading saxophonists of James Brown's band, Maceo Parker and Fred Wesley— literally announced the planetary departure to the *Fourth World* on the mothership, with not one earthbound mellow love song.

The emergence of technofunk is not simply a repetition of black escapism nor an adolescent obsession with star trek; technofunk constitutes the second grand break of Afro-American popular music. Like Charlie Parker's bebop, George Clinton's technofunk both Africanizes and technologizes Afro-American popular music—with polyrhythms on polyrhythms, less melody and freaky electronically distorted vocals. Similar to bebop, a technofunk unabashedly exacerbates and accentuates the blackness of black music, the Afro-Americanness of Afro-American music— its irreducibility, inimitability and uniqueness. Funkadelic and Parliament defy nonblack emulation; they assert their distinctiveness—and the distinctiveness of funk in Afro-America. This funk is neither a skill nor an idea, nor a worldview or a stance. Rather it is an existential capacity to get in touch with forms of kinetic orality and emotional physicality acquired by deep entrenchment in the patterns of Afro-American ways of life and struggle.

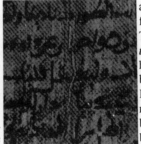

For black technofunk, in a period of increasing black strata and class divisions, there are no fundamental cleavages in Afro-American, only the Black Nation. The cover of George Clinton's 1978 Funkadelic album, *One Na-tion Under A Groove,* portrays black folk from all walks of life hoisting up Marcus Garvey's Afro-American liberation flag (of red, blackand green stripes) with R & B printed on it—the initials not for Rhythm and Blues but Rhythm and Business. In vintage black nationalist patriarchal fashion, the inside of the album contains a beautiful naked black woman lying on her back signifying the biological source and social backbone of the Black Nation. Like bebop, technofunk's breakthrough was brief. Its intensely Africanizing and technologizing thrust was quickly diluted and brought more and more into contact with other nonblack musical currents, as witnessed in Prince's creative Minneapolis sound and Midnight Star's freakazoid funk.

The distinctive talent of Michael Jackson is that he combines the performative showmanship of James Brown (whom he imitated in his first 1969 exhibited to gain a contract with Motown), the lyrical emotional intensity of Smokey Robinson, the trans-racial appeal of Dionne Warwicke and the aggressive though attenuated technofunk of The Isley Brothers. Michael Jackson is the musical dynamo of his generation. This became quite clear with his highly-acclaimed 1979 *Off The Wall* album and further confirmed by his records-setting 1982 *Thriller.* Like Muhammed Ali—and unlike most of his musical contemporaries—Michael Jackson is an international star of grand proportions, the most prominent world-historical emblem of the Afro-American spiritual-blues impulse. Ironically, and unlike the only other comparable figure, Louis Armstrong, Michael Jackson is not a musical revolutionary within Afro-American history. Rather he is a funnel. It is precisely his versatility and diversity—from old funk, technofunk, mellow soul to ballads with the ex-Beatle, Paul McCartney—which marks his protean musical identity.

The Black Church, black owned and black run Christian congregations, is the fountain head of the Afro-American spiritual-blues impulse. Yet, as should be apparent, the Black Church has suffered tremendous artistic drainage. The giant talents of Mahalia Jackson, James Cleveland and Clara Ward prove that the Black Church can keep some of its sons and daughters in the artistic fold, but for every one who stayed with the gospels, there have been four who went to Rhythm and Blues. In the late sixties, Edwin Hawkins' *Oh Happy Day* received national visibility, but the gospel explosion—partly spawned by the Pentecostal thrust in the black religious community—did not take off until the reunion of James Cleveland and Aretha Franklin in their historic 1972 double album-set *Amazing Grace*. The towering success of this live concert at the New Temple Missionary Baptist Church in Los Angeles convinced many reluctant recording companies that gospel music was marketable. And soon superb albums such as Andrae Couch's *Take Me Back,* Walter Hawkins' (Edwin's brother) *Love Alive* and *Love Alive II* proved them correct. Although gospel music remains primarily a black affair—written and performed by and for black people— the recent Christian conversions of the popular Deneice Williams and disco queen Donna Summers may broaden the scope.

The most important development in Afro-American popular music since 1979 is black rap music. This music has been performed on ghetto streets and between stage acts during black concerts for many years. In 1979, Sylvia Robinson, the major songwriter for the mellow soul group, *The Moments* (recently renamed Ray, Goodman and Brown), decided to record and release *Rapper's Delight* by Harlem's Sugarhill Gang. Within months, black rap records were filling record shops around the country. Most of the first black rap records were musically derived from big hits already released and lyrically related to adolescent love affairs. Yet as more sophisticated rap performers, such as Kurtis Blow and Grandmaster Flash and the Furious Five emerged, the music became more original and the lyrics more graphic of life in the black ghetto. Kurtis Blow's *The Breaks* and *125th Street* and Grandmaster Flash and the Furious Five's *The Message* and *New York, New York* are exemplary in this regard.

Black rap music is more important than the cross-over of jazz musicians to Rhythm and Blues, the rise of the 'older' Michael Jackson and the return of gospel music because, similar to bebop and technofunk, black rap music is emblematically symptomatic of a shift in sensibilities and moods in Afro-America. Black rap music indeed Africanizes Afro-American popular music—accenting syncopated polyrhythms, kinetic orality and sensual energy in a refined form of raw expressiveness—while its virtuosity lies not in technical facility but rather in street-talk quickness and linguistic versality. In this sense, like bebop and technofunk, black rap music resists nonblack reproduction, though such imitations and emulations proliferate. The major predecessors of black rap music were the political raps of Gil-Scott Heron and the powerful musical poems of The Last Poets over a decade ago; their content was angry, funky and hopeful. Black rap music is surely grounded in the Afro-American spiritual-blues impulse, but certain versions of this music radically calls into question the roots of this impulse, the roots of transcendence and opposition. The roots of the Afro-American and spiritual-blues impulse are in the supposition that somebody cares. Black rap music challenges this supposition—the future of the Afro-American spiritual-blues tradition may well hang on the quality of the response to this challenge.

Too Early Too Late

Arnold Barkus

The time comes when everything has already been seen. There is traffic in the streets, the economy is normal; in the countryside farmers are forgotten and rewarded. There is no lack of things. On the contrary, there are more and more things. Nor has there been any loss of light. Only strange visitors and planes passing overhead might notice a certain dimness. New coats of paint, hardly dry, shine in the daylight before another coat is added.

The fashions of the entire century are worn to celebrate the richness of the present. Books are read as if they had already been read before; streets, buildings, fields, all spaces are approached as if they had already been approached before. Jokes are laughed at as they are about to be spoken. The most startling tricks of the magican fail to surprise. Adults tell children little of what they know, less of what they don't know. Politicians retain power but lose crowds. The law applies to those who are ignorant but only partially to those who are insane, but the guilty part makes all the difference between yes and no.

Everything runs on time because nothing is off. People leave in the middle of things because there is no question of what had happened. People are simply absent from the middle of things because they left the middle behind earlier on. Time passes like this.

Most everyone seems to have something to sell. Some keep it buried away. There are madmen on the street, but a madman is not a madman if he is in a group of two or more. There are not many people who want to share. Nobody has anything to spare. All is expendable. One holds on to what one has long after it has disappeared. When one gives one does so in an act of taking. And defiance is an act of deference. Violence against inanimate objects is not uncommon. Violence of objects against people goes virtually unnoticed. Those with weapons wrap themselves around them, become them. Blood spills, and no one sees it turn to water. It is always too early, already too late. Each person's wish remains bound to its opposite. Whole autopsies are performed in public. The desire to strip the body of its interior mysteries is never satisfied. A form of suicide becomes popular in which the entire body is turned inside out. But, at the same time, people heal with auto-surgery. Poets and painters replace faces and landscapes with organs. X-rays replace photographs inside the wallet.

The division of the sexes has never been more marked, though never before have men and women been so exchangeable, one for the other. Buildings continue to soar upward, the privileged live in the clouds, the old paradigm of heaven and hell is reincarnated in the architecture of the skyscraper, though the top and bottom floors are in some ways duplicates of each other. Men take to the streets leaving women passengers behind in their automobiles, and women do the same; they shout at each other. Prostitutes refuse to be Johned and instead steal the caps of traffic policemen and direct vehicles into head-on collisions. The radio broadcasts make the suitable announce-

95

ments: traffic jams, grid lock, road spills, dump sites, major wars, unnatural disasters and renewed hatred between heads of state and whole populations.

On this planet there is no longer any common sky. What was once called nature has been replaced by outer space. But the old problems are not replaced and the new outside looks exactly the same as the old inside. The bodies of our characters are driven toward the clean vacuum of space and the electronics of a new nervous system. The monsters really are more horrifying than anything we'd seen on earth because they are made that way. But outer space remains and is constantly recreated by the turn toward its invisible threat, its blackness, sometimes blinding brightness, its silence and its roar. People are seduced by it, and begin to look like it, because they look into it and are filled by it. They breathe in a vacuum and still hear their own breath, though they may be very far away from it.

The camera observes them; constructing bridges, putting together the pieces of a satellite system of secret dimensions, moving objects around, objects which have no weight, which fail to fall from the hand, receiving codes to be inserted into a computer which has not yet been programmed. They wear costumes of the period, smoke cigarettes of the interplanetary design.

Tomorrow we will land on the planet X. And we will stay where we stayed last year this time. But we do not expect to recognize any of the old faces or the places we haunted. We move from day to day.

We are making a film in which the characters are to become invisible and it is the funniest task because it is we who shoot and watch the film who seek this invisibility and by the disappearance of our film characters we suddenly rediscover our flesh, become visible to a degree we never though we could bear. We walk on a floor which travels at the speed of light, we think thoughts while looking out a window which travels at the speed of light, we are still waiting as we travel at the speed of light toward a goal which has already come to meet us. It is the same day. I don't remember the planets and the stars by their given names but recall the architecture of this space which folds over on itself, yet permits continuation. Erotic architecture which leaves us laughing.

Later, we go walking in the street, and pick up objects with our hands, anything that isn't nailed to the ground, and then put them down again. By daybreak, the entire city has been tampered with.

for Jean-Marie Straub and Danielle Huillet

A Modern Way to Die

Peter Wortsman

Once there was a war that no one could see. No bombs exploded. Nobody shrieked. People just dropped dead suddenly. Inexplicably. In the kitchen, in the bedroom, on their weary way home from work. Some said it was heart attack, but too many succumbed to the mysterious affliction for that theory to hold. Others swore it was something in the air: a poison wind from the east, a cosmic inversion.

Though never openly discussed—*cloudy weather* was the favored euphemism—everyone secretly feared being next, and there were those who went so far as to wish it, just to put an end to the unendurable anxiety. But man has an uncanny ability to adapt and make the best of things.

Children started the game, adults followed suit, and soon everyone was at it, picking out prospective victims from the 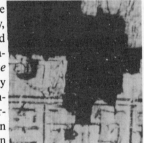 crowd. The talented few, able to point with a deadly accuracy, earned the epithet *golden fin-gered,* and the best of these could command sizable fees to perform in public. Concert halls and sta- diums were hired. People flocked to see their favorites. *Prize Fingers,* as the papers liked to call them, were invariably shorter than their poster effigies, and despite the blindfold (govern- ment regulations), they strode confidently straight to center- stage. Some went in for arabesque antics: twists and turns, and Latin incantations—but the truly great worked with sparse gestures in absolute silence.

A raised palm hushed the crowd. The thumb and three fingers bowed, and the forefinger seemed to grow as it swept out over the sea of anxious eyes, drawn like a compass to the next malignant north. Sometimes a skuffle ensued — the way baseball fans struggle for possession of a home-run or a foul, only in reverse: nobody wanted to catch it. But the issue rapidly resolved itself (to the wild delight of spectators) with a sudden squirm and a frenetic hiss, like that of air leaving a balloon. Ushers carted off the corpse, and those seated the closest wiped the sweat off their brows and invariably claimed they'd had their eye on him or her from the start.

Of course there were fakes, as there are in every art, individuals lacking in any genuine talent who climb the latest bandwagon for fame and fortune. They hide behind a lot of hocus pocus, — and rumor had it that certain charlatans stooped so low as to plant hitmen in the audience to discreetly dispose of predesignated targets on cue.

A great favorite, whose reputation is still the subject of some debate, had black eyes and a finger that drove the women wild. Old maids and teenage girls alike swooned at the sight of him.

Ladies!...gentlemen! he whispered, the microphone turned up to capacity, *Look your neighbor in the eye! Can you see! Can you tell! Who is going to be next?* Married women shivered, husbands studied their wives, even young lovers regarded each other with new interest.

Take me!...Take me! cried the most fervent fans, as the drumroll marked the moment.

What followed at one particular performance has become legend. Eyewitnesses swear that a little boy high up in the bleechers broke the shell of silence. *Heh, Mister!* he cried out, but the master had reached the climax of his act and refused to be disturbed. People tried to still the child. The drumroll swelled, the master's finger swayed. *Mister!* the little boy yelled—heads turned in shock and wonder at the child's audacity—*Mister!* he called, ***you're next!***

Stage hands later confirmed how they saw the prize finger tremble and turn white, how one clasped the microphone while the other tore off the blindfold, and the crowd's black-eyed darling crumbled to the floor of the stage.

Critics had a heyday, unanimously lambasting the deceased, who had been popular too long, and hailing the boy as a fresh new talent. The incident flickered on in the news till a colorful murder case preempted the spotlight. The boy was said to have made something of a career for himself overseas.

Nowadays, outside of a small circle of die hards, nobody pays much attention to the art anymore. Death has become such a common occurrence that the thrill of guessing has gone out of it. Live combat is back in fashion — war as vivid and spectacular as it once was. People missed the epic sweep and the glorious bang of the bomb.

Skin Deep

Damona Wolff

In the quarrys, deep in the dig, there's no chance to love work, only sweat, the sweat glistens with the comforting promise of body salve to soften the muscles hardened in the quarry, muscles aching from the relentless penetrations of hard science. Is it a real diamond this time, is it the Last Equation, is it iron ore, is it Brain Power? The **SWEAT GLAND** is a gland I can live with, a gland I can't love without, though at the moment it's bone dry in the quarry, deep in the dig, and I am longing for the GOLGI CORPUSCLE. Leaning against my cold rolled probe, I remember the history lessons, when our whole species history, our hole history—digging in, digging out—ran like hot blood through my veins; to tap the steaming stream I had only to peel back the **EPIDERMIS** ever so lightly. Then the dead cells started piling up faster than I could peel. Every introspection, every dig in session, uncovered only skin, more skin, layer after layer pressed together into keratin pastry substituting for the earth's crust: the skin of dispersion and refusal, the skin of inquisition, the skin that got away, the skin they flayed away, requisitioned skin, prostitution skin, burnt skin, brazen skin, ancient skin, trade-in toxic skin (just look at the callouses) and over there, just beneath the crisp wafer skin of extinction, the dark leather skin of a **MASTODON** *Though Mother may be short on arms, her skin is full of warmth and charms, and Mother's touch on baby's skin, endears the heart that beats within.* We soon discovered that while skin was piling up all over the planet, each nation had its naming layers, a distinct mode of compression and a certain national depth. Here, in the United States (one of the more troublesome digs), the crust is thick with red skin, beaver skin, whole economies of skin. We once unearthed a massive library of brittle history books, each bound in skin—slave skin, red skin, the skin of all those who made it the wrong way, skins that never made it at all. Years of scraping away in the U.S. dig make me want to sample the European crust, mostly so as to have a glimpse at the portrait of **THE WOLFMAN OF MUNICH**, still hanging in the partially excavated Castle Ambras, the very same portrait given by Strauss, Duke of Bavaria, to his Uncle Ferdinand, who loved grisly displays and long objects of aggression. So here is Petrus Gonsalvus, the Wolfman of Munich, a born terrorist, victim of a hideous disease called **DERMITOLOGY,** though some say he made the ladies giggle with delight in Paris, and it is certainly true that throughout all of Europe, the Wolfman of Munich was admired for the truly spectacular dimensions of his **PACINIAN CORPUSCLE.** It used to be a commonplace: the Word was a body, writing a hand, the hand a touch and touch meant skin. The consensus did not hold. Hard scientists, shunning the secretive pleasures of the surface, wanted to get deeper, and for this they invented dissection, and for this they manufactured corpses. As they held their hyperhygienic festivals of textual penetration, a dissident faction split off in hommage to the **RHINOCEROUS** *The Rhino's skin is thick and tough, yet the skin is soft enough that baby Rhinos always sense a love enormous and intense.* The hard scientists didn't seem to notice the scars left behind by their ambitious surgery, and soon the body of the Word, the once immaculate body of the Word, looked exactly like the rest of the planet, some wounds closed with hardened scar tissue, others open, sore, staring blankly at the research teams who in turn hunted feverishly for a fresh place to cut. It was during these times that I learned to measure the tremors induced by the **CORPUSCLE OF RUFFINI,** as the surface of the planet became coated with ashes, ashes firing up from half- clotted pores, jammed tunnels and vengeful volcanos, firing, drifting, settling; ashes piled up everywhere as the air crackled with transmissions assuring the fate of commodity futures and mustard gas. The planetary skin grew course and black, it was hard not to notice, even for the lusty Senators who sat in their saunas scrubbing their skin, wondering what is this itch and where does it come from? This time, darkness really was in the air, and our choice was a simple one: join the dead flow ash drift or lay gifts of penance at the hastily constructed temple honoring the **CORPUSCLE OF KRAUSS,** the oracle corpuscle, the only corpuscle that could tell us what we needed to know. I assure you that when the world gets colder, nothing is any longer a question of attitude, the skin is chilled, touch it and your fingers drop off like a popsicle from the stick, try to lick the cold wound with the warmth of your lips, but they too are gone, your teeth have chattered off your most special skin into oblivion, so you do nothing oral, know nothing oral for the hole of time except, that is, to watch **MESSNER'S CORPUSCLE** dry out. By that time, it's much too late to be so penetrating as to write the true history of species interiors because, you see, the skin would not hold. Even when nothing could be touched anymore, all was held permissible in matters of the surface. Then the mutations caught up with us; the skin festered, hardened, scaled. So *this* was the species that had probed so deeply as to jump clear out of its skin, now that's *real* lava flowing through the veins, and it's hot but not inviting, unlike the skin of the **PELVIS.** Hard science gave us the news; the pelvis was the last habitable territory on the face of the Earth, and this had not to do with reproduction but with habitat, not with passion but with microbes, bacteria, parasites, there, in the cradle of civilization. **MELANOCYTES** continued to churn out pigment. The desert was expanding and Isis laughed (how I love it when she laughs) as the species dug in for the duration and began to fashion for itself the skin of a **SNAKE** *To baby vipers, scaly skin engenders love 'twixt kith and kin, each animal by God is blessed with kind of skin it loves the best.* Meanwhile, we all gathered around the last remaining monolith, **MERKEL'S CORPUSCLE,** and recalled the time when women said our skin is softer than yours and men said so what. Now we stand here together, deep in the dig, and there's no chance to love work. Bone dry and without lips, we trace in the dirt with our hard science probes the makings of a legend for the future, when the benefactors of our mutations heat up debates over the rumor of sensation. Yes, there was such a thing; we called it **SKIN.**

Scent

Marylène Delbourg-Delphis

Perfume is an open air art. Each of its elements—flask, packing, scent, advertisement—generates and multiplies illusions. Constellation upon constellation, the perfumed universe would be Aragon's Novel-Theater in search of a cast, if it weren't for all these women here in the flesh, with all their nostrils, all their particularities. Looked at from the perspective of the Novel-Theater, the six thousand brands of perfume distributed in France over the past one hundred years appear as so many titles in a vast imaginary library. *Yasmak, Le Ming, Daimo, Afgani, Secret de Sphinx, Shalimar, Nuit de Chine, Vol de Nuit, don't you feel Chantilly today?*

It is not the role of perfume to exhibit love by means of a phenomena of contamination or identification comparable to the dirty mirrors of erotic literature; rather, perfume stimulates processes while at the same time 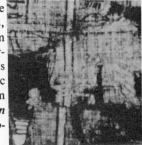 assuring their paralysis in the cliche. Perfume never comes, never procreates. Perfume arouses desires only to put them back to sleep. This motionless escape, an escape through inter-ruption, is the beginning of a dreaming process that seems always to return to its source. In such a scenario, both domestic stability and institutionalized hope convey a kind of boredom that courts failure. *Le Secret de Lulu, Toujours Moi, Amour en Cage, Balcon, Heure Exquise, Le Dandy, Arpège, Vertige, Cabo-chard, Remember the name, you will never forget the fragrance.*

The library is divided into sections, issuing visas for every kind of other life. The heroine in this series of episodes is the woman, the same woman who one might try to grasp, yet she is elsewhere, finding refuge in a double, in a substitute. Perfume becomes, as advertised for Lancome's *Climat* (1967), the *pure presence of an absent woman.* Sustained by her double and by means of ritualistic effects, our heroine abandons herself to the pleasures of ornament, to elegant ceremonials, and secret worships.

Obviously, there is a history to perfume. In 1983, a woman no longer desires *brown and sugared Cyprus,* favorite of Colette's heroine Claudine. It is also clear, however, that many perfumes escape time and become classics. At any given moment, they match what scent can accept. They have the strength of certain works of art, they have no history because they have anticipated in their substance the whole of the nose. *Shocking You, Must du Jour, Chanel 5, Infini, Espaces, Envol, Complice, Ramage, Christalle.* One is tempted to say that the nose can do without history. It always returns to square one, and sometimes simply gets tired out. The nose forgets its passions as quickly as that which it rejects. It is because perfume can be so *lethal* that lasting scents become exemplary witnesses of an epoch. They are symbols of the moment in which they were first sniffed, and from which they escaped.   *Coriandre; the perfume that makes one question the value of civilization.*

translation by Brigitte Ouvry-Vial and Damona Wolff

Denizen of the Universe

Frank Ungemut

Entropy will end the world   The world will end ineluctably in a state of total chaos. The more time passes, the more the disorder increases. It is the world's inexorable course towards destruction; life being only a topical fight, intense but inefficacious, against the spread of decay. *The physical law governing the increase of entropy has considerably heightened the pessimist's fatalistic vision of universal history.* Physical meaning: energetic homogenization as well as maximum spatial disorder. That is the overall perspective. Entropy as a concept within physics and the application that concept as an idea by non-physicists, e.g. Ernst Bloch, when talking about entropy on an astronomical scale and the end of our planetary system, the collapse of the sun, the illustration of the nothing, *le neant, Nichts.* Bloch elaborates further on the idea of Armageddon; Christ will come back to earth for the new Jerusalem to shine as the only source of light after the vanishing of sun and moon. A utopian idea working against the concept of entropy.

The application of entropy to sociology.   One could associate the wealth of each individual with the level of energetic excitation of each particle. Energetic homogenization would mean that each person would have the same economic level without implying uniformity of one's basic nature. Maximum spatial disorder would enable each person to be at any given place at any given moment. Politically speaking, this would mean total freedom of movement for everyone, without reference to a central information network.

A new model of politics—Build an organic computer into the human body   In an organic computer the logic switches consist of molecules which can exist in two states, 0 or 1, representing a bit. Naturally occurring substances—such as a component of hemoglobin—exhibit the necessary property. To get information into and out of a computer tiny wires can be used that are themselves made out of chemicals. Certain polymers, which are chain-structured chemicals, can conduct electricity. Genetically manipulated bacteria could produce a protein that would form the skeleton of the computer. This progein would have specific sites to which the various molecular components would adhere, enabling the computer to assemble itself, much as nature assembles biological substances. But one could even deposit tiny lines of silver on a one-molecule-thick layer of protein. All problems connecting an organic computer to an electric periphery could be evaded immediately. The human mind is the final addressee anyway, or would it create humans who become carriers for computers? On the other hand, computing structures could be produced which must be programmed by means of external storage devices, i.e. the organic computer could be hooked into big main frame machines, to provide temporary programming which could then be replaced. Such is the fantasy of the perfect slave. But it turns out that this is not an artificial humanoid but the manipulated human being itself, a mutation (in the full meaning of the word in Latin *mutare* — to go forward and to spread something, also to change, to exchange, even to do business, to trade, to barter; moreover to alter, to transform and to tune).

So ultimately the genetic code for production could be implanted into the human genetic material; a new internal organ becomes part of these mutants, indeed several new internal organs which either produce the computing structure and also produce replacement parts for repair or which constitute the computing structure itself, a second brain so to speak, since it becomes increasingly clear that the regular human brain does not work like a digital computer (ironically there is the attempt to match computing machines with the intellectual structure of the brain, with its reflective capacities, while it seems to turn out that the basic principle of the computer, the 0-1 binary code, is not applicable to the functioning of brainpower nor is human thinking, the associative, creative mode transferable to any machine structure). The ideal computer carrier (CC) would be found in highly qualified programmers who then could program the organic computer, the other internal organ in their bodies. The intellectual effort of programmers could be directly connected and applied to the computing structure, thus the programmer's brain functions as a transforming device, i.e. receiving information, orders from external people and media in general and shaping this for feeding into the computing structure. The mind of a CC could hold particular functional tasks to intervene in regard to programming questions. This is then the production of a new kind of human being, not a new race but more of a mutation (comparable to so-called *mongoloids* who happen to have one additional gene in their set of genetic material). It opens unexpected opportunities.

The result of the comput- **ing process** To read other people's minds.

Scenario I Here is a plot imaginable where space-travellers come to planet Earth finding the remains of a once highly developed civilization. After an exten- sive investigation of the planet they find out that a long time ago their ancestors came from the same planet but their civilization did not survive.

Scenario II Two bacteria orbit around the planet Earth, each of them in a satellite. Each bacteria represents one of the two dominating blocs on Earth. Do bacteria have morals? When hungry they gobble pickled algae, providing the main frame computer on Earth with the necessary instructions, which are indeed the decisions made to rule the people. The bacteria is the host for the computing structure, produces the frame structure and assembles with protein the organic computer. The bacteria is a quasi-factory for one computer unit, built, maintained and run by way of a vital creature. The bacteria could influence the computing structure, could impose its bacterial will and desire to the commands that ultimately govern the humans. What could one expect from a bacteria? Fundamental organic aspirations, but we know that this kind of fundamentalism is not right for people.

Quantizing gravity *The last adventure in theory,* the closing of the gap between the inneratomic forces and gravity.

Unifying-pacifying?

The blink of an eye   This moment when everything vanishes into a big black hole and immediately explodes in a big bang, this moment of infinite shrinkage when time and space disappear in a pinpoint, this moment?

Talking about the universe   —but not knowing how people feel about relationships —euphemism of the white race —the unspeakable truth of Western living.

The theological aspect   *The Roman Catholic church seems to be very happy with the idea of the big bang,* says Hawking.

Images   What ideas and feelings become related to these phenomena of cosmic dimension; the black holes, stars being swallowed by each other, the big bang and its counterpart, the big end at the time, the numerical dimension: be it timespans of 20,000 millions years or 10^{-35} seconds, 10^{16} suns, 10^{23} cubic light-years of space; one light-year equals some billion miles; numbers for meditational purposes, transcendental feelings occur. We have descriptions of cosmic events that, being transposed into human dimensions surpass all atrocities know so far. It is very unlikely that such events will happen during human existence, but nevertheless, even if the probability is very tiny, still it might happen . . . something.

Big Bang theory

—large scale structure of the universe.
—filamental structure of cosmic matter.
—dark matter. i.e. invisible between bright matter, might be predominant.
—halos of invisible matter around galaxies.
—the massive neutrino; i.e. neutrinos were long believed to have any mass at all (even if the neutrino should prove to have zero mass it does not invalidate the pancake theory), new assessments make it very likely that neutrinos have a very little mass, 10–20 eV (i.e. less than ten thousandth of an electron mass) which ultimately would add up to an enormous mass in the sense of an invisible mass with very slow movement and very weak interaction, very neutral matter, almost negligible when occurring as single bodies but in its vast quantities it is very necessary to take it in account.
—dark matter may comprise 90% of the mass of the universe (here the parallel to the masses in social theory comes along)
—the dynamics of the structure: I. isolated pancakes, II. Cellular structure of neighboring pancakes, III. dissipating or disappearance of cellular structure.

Cosmological models and social perspective   1) Assuming a direct relationship between the two fields. 2) in a historical perspective: a. finds models for I. cosmological theories. II. social prospects. b. is an historical sequence detectable in both field? 2aI) *grand unified theories* 1980's —peace movement, ecology movement, *entropy* 1950's death, pessimism, anticommunism, see: Entropy as a model for sociology. 2aI)&b) Do these models build on the predecessor, i.e. is there a continuity and further is there any imaginable future model based on present and past models, or are there discontinuities, e.g. the mediaeval Christian model of the flat disc which was challenged by Copernicus etc.? Would there have been a completely new approach with the abolition of private property? 3) Computation about the fate of the universe within the big bang theory, i.e. what happened in the very beginning, the first micro-seconds etc., and what will happen towards the end, an anticipated timespan that exceeds all human dimension. Draw parallels between three models: I) filamental structure of the universe. II a) cellular structure of life tissue. b) filamental structure of cell-interior. III) social relations as a filamental structure between people.

The structure of the universe   The Shane-Wirtanen Survey shows a vast network of clusters, filaments and voids, altogether one million galaxies. This segment of the sky shows on paper a remarkable structure. Where the cosmologists search for concentrations, holes and tissue-material there opens a picture of completely unexpected complexity. *The human eye can see patterns in random dots.* And this firmament reveals rich patterns; when our ancestors looked up to the stars they saw the same thing.

The Future of the Universe   If the density is equal to or greater than a critical density, which is about three protons for every 1000 liters of space, gravity will eventually overcome the expansion and the universe will collapse. A forecast of the expanding universe through the year 10^{100}:

All protons will decay, galaxies will form black holes and black holes will evaporate. If the universe collapses, it may cycle into an infinity of error.

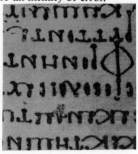

Klong Toey

Alphonso Lingis

In the shifting wastelands beyond the pyramids, gnostics watched the Egyptian night. In the wastes beyond Alexandria and Thebes, the gnostic was not a surveyor, a lookout or a spy. The gnostics, insomniac, watched the night with a sense of disaster, of the stars burning out and of the lukewarm cinder of a planet vaporizing into cold dust, burning out into night. The gnostic nightwatch insomnia was a deathwatch, a peer into the spaces of disaster; so, this is compassion. The bhikku who is said to have said *I am myself a dream* was not a skeptic; he had simply come to see the day with the eyes of an insomniac. His wakefulness had neither aim nor desire. He was silent out of shame, tracing the tracks of the snow leopard. And so I tell myself, I must be patient.

Klong Toey Outside 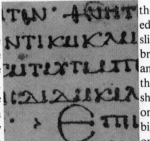 the drizzle continued. The air was still, and the rain had not cooled it at all. The wetness cleaned nothing, and the humidity made slime bead on one's limbs and on the bars of the cages. The trustie brought in the morning's food, an aluminum plate of plain rice and a coffee can of water. I tried to eat the rice with my fingers, the right hand only, for the left is for washing after defecating. One should use the first three fingers only, and the food should touch only the first joints of the fingers. But I was able to lift only big pinches this way, and a third of it was dropping each time back on the plate I held under my chin. I watched your fingers deftly efficient. I thought: a plate of plain rice, no doubt most of the meals in your life had been that. Your stomach was flat and tight, under your chest sprung broad. Did you spend all your childhood in the cotton mill? I asked. *No. After a year they came and took me, and put me in a massage house for men.* Owned also by the Chinese? *No. The owner was a colonel in the army.* Did you ever see him? *He took me the first night.* Did you ever see your family again? *When I was fourteen.* Did you stay there then? *I went to steal guns. After two weeks I got caught.* You broke into a store? *No. I and two others waited for an officer outside the base. He picked me up the second night. When he was asleep I took his gun and his money. A week later he recognized me in the bazaar and grabbed me. He told the police I lifted his gun in the crowded bazaar. I told them he had picked me up to fuck me. I described his bedroom to them, and his underwear. They locked me up in Khon Kaen.* You lay down too on the floor near me. In the light of the bare bulb I suddenly saw your hand: you are missing a finger on the right hand. The trigger finger. During the war hundreds of communist sympathizers chopped off their trigger fingers to avoid induction into the army.

Pungkaeow I watched her fingers, animated with schemes of their own, break and stir the food. She spoke no English. I went through my repertoire of stock conversations in Thai with her, and she, very engrossed in this, taught me some new expressions. Whatever she did she kept a hand in yours, or a leg in contact with yours, as though she had to draw animal spirits from your organism in order to even talk. I used the chain she wore about her neck as an alibi to touch her; I lifted it and saw it held a blue sapphire. I looked at it closely, feeling the delicate movements in her throat like ripples simmering on a summer pond. She turned back to you and held up the chain you wore; it had a black star sapphire on it. She ran her fingers lightly over the corridors of the intricate tattoo in blue lines that covered your chest, and began to read the ciphers, pronouncing them one by one, like mantras. What did that mean, I asked. You did not know how to translate it for me. Perhaps for you they were mantras, and not statements. It is for protection, you said. The tattoo covered your heart.

Finally the muddy dawn came, and the guards turned off the lights and opened the monkey cages so that we could go to the toilet. Before the sink I studied my yellowing jaundiced abdomen. You came back with Puangkaeow. I saw her downless creamy stomach through her half-buttoned blouse. Her huge black eyes slid in their gleaming fluids like primitive marine animals turned unblinking on me. She had lumps of foods in a thin pink plastic bag which clung like skin to the packets it held. Your body was mesomorphe without looking tumescent and without angular movements, as though it had this virile shape by being formed in a mold. It seemed to me that it was youth alone that maintained this shape, despite the lack of solid food, despite the lack of exercise in these cages for how many years now. I tried to imagine how you would look when you got fat, middle-aged and bald. I tried to imagine you then, as now, hovering over me, arranging a bed for me. There was something missing in this maternal image—your finger. Your finger, that which could stiffen, probe, penetrate—in what male contest did you loose it? The trustie came to lock the cages for the day; Puangkaeow went to him and spoke with him; he let her stay. We smoked again, the sour smoke churned in the bile inside my wet body and I felt not the soothing torpor of sleep coming on, but the ebbing away of my forces. I lay back on the floor. She bent over me and began to massage my feet and legs, Siamese massage, applying hard thumb points of pressure to stop and release the blood in the veins. Then she worked on my arms. When she turned to my chest, I took her in my hands and pulled her down on me. How much passion this frail girl who could not speak a word of my language had in her incarcerated body. As she poured it upon me I was aware of a black pool of hatred beneath the ardent torpor that floated in my body, a hatred directed at you.

The next day the vice-consul came with an interpreter. He gave me a list of lawyers. The first on the list, he said, was intelligent enough to have graduated fifth in her class at Thamassat Law School five years ago. She is married to an inspector of police. He bailed me out to the hospital. Two days later I was sentenced by the court to pay a fine of 200 baht, and be expelled from the country within twenty-four hours. I saw the little man with the tense, twisted ears who had planted the dope on me standing at the back of the courtroom; my lawyer said he would receive 50% of the fine. She accompanied me back to the monkey cages of Klong Toey to pay the bail; I also bought ten cartons of cigarettes. I had to stand there with her to insist that the guards really passed them through the bars. They saw me. They will think now, I thought hopelessly, that the American was a good guy. They will generalize. But we had *all* been there because of the Americans. The hill tribes of the Himalayan foothills, living off slash and burn agriculture in the jungle, had always used some of the opium that grows wild there, as Chinese old people use opium, as the aged in Morocco smoke kiff. During the war the CIA contacted the remnants of the Kuomintang

Army which had been in the Golden Triangle in southern Burma and northern Thailand since the flight of Chiang Kai-Shek to Taiwan, and contracted them to supply opium to finance recruitment of saboteurs among the hill tribes of Vietnam and Laos. The generals of Saigon skimmed off rich profits from this trade, notably air marshal Nguyen Cao Key, who controlled the flights. When in the final days of the war the American troops were being shipped home, anxiety of heroin addiction among them, returning to the jobless slums, was a matter of serious concern in Washington. It was impossible to intercept heroin in the innumerable lines of shipment; the only possibility was to try to cut off production at the sources. The Nixon government then arranged a large grant of money and equipment to Thailand to wipe out production of heroin in the Golden Triangle. But this money was given to the military junta installed in Bangkok, whose attention was devoted less to government or even to defense than to the exploitation of the resources of the country to swell bank accounts abroad. The rules would rejoin when Thailand too fell to the advancing Viet armies. Profits from the heroin industry was an essential part of their income. The anti-narcotics investment then made it necessary to arrest a certain quantity of peddlers and smugglers. Rather than send the ill-paid troops into the mountain strongholds of heroin warlords, they had the police in Bangkok employ informers, addicts themselves, to entrap novice smugglers. The Thais are a proud people, the only country in southern Asia to have never been subjugated by European imperialism. They resent being treated by foreigners as a land of addicts responsible for the drugging of American youth in the slums of the richest nation on the planet. To make this point they arrest a certain number of Americans. And I, good guy passing through Klong Toey, was dissembling what I am with my cigarettes of tobacco.

Thon Buri The following winter I went to Papau New Guinea and Java for three months; when my Indonesian visa ran out I still had 18 days left before I had to return. I learned that one could enter Thailand without a visa if one had a paid ticket for departure within fourteen days. I now had two weeks to find you. I first contacted the lawyer; she had indeed received my wire of funds and had obtained the release of Puangkaeow, who was now working in a factory in Thon Buri. The following day I went with the lawyer to the factory. We waited for the end of the work shift. The foreman brought Puangkaeow, who greeted us formally and timidly. We sat down on stools at a soup stall in an alley near the klong. She told me that you had jumped off a roof to kill yourself. Soon after I had left, on the night of the first full moon. The roof of a two story building. For there are no buildings high enough, as in the rich cities of my country, for the poor of Thon Buri to dash themselves into instantaneous death. You had jumped from the roof of a two story building. It had taken three days for you to die.

Puangkaeow's fingers rested by her side; her face was utterly still. Her black eyes were opaque, and began to glisten. Slowly it began to rain.

KA

Bahadur Tejani

To the outsider who tries to understand the secrets of the Sahara, the sun is a powerful psychological and physical threat. But to the thousands of Berbers, Tuaregs, Hausa and Fulani traders who live in or around the desert, it is the opposite. The sun is not merely a friend but the pivot point of their daily life. In the metaphysical world of the Muslim, a believer creates symbolic unity between the sky and the earth five times a day, guided by the position of the sun. In his inner life the sun is therefore an integral part of the cosmic order guiding the believer's steps and his prayers leading to the fulfillment of the daily cycle of light and darkness. One has only to witness the bare-headed sons of the Sahara trading in the noon day sun in today's marketplace, abandoning their business to bow their heads in worship on the burning cement or sizzling sand, to realize that the sun god is not a threat to their life. Every muslim must look at the sun squarely in the eye and face the East before beginning worship.

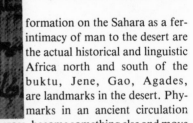

The ancient historical information on the Sahara as a fertile area and the psychological intimacy of man to the desert are stimulating thoughts leading to the actual historical and linguistic evidence of exchange between Africa north and south of the Sahara. Fabled cities like Timbuktu, Jene, Gao, Agades, Audoghost, Fez and Marakech are landmarks in the desert. Physical landmarks, but also landmarks in an ancient circulation of the Word, sites where every African tongue could enter, cross, become something else and move on. We can survey the topography of this connectedness by turning our ears to the continent as it names itself.

The Egyptians tried to endow both the physical body and psychic life of a person with immortality. Their techniques of embalming and preservation are legendary but not enough attention is given to the creation and spread of the metaphysical term defined as *Ka*. This was regarded as the spirit or the second self of a person denoting his vital energy. A person was born with a *Ka* unique to oneself, a companion even in one's journey through the world of the dead.

Ka may be found spread in so many places, contexts and persons that it indicates a certain underlying unity. The most important shrine of the muslim world in Mecca is called the *Kaba* in Saudi Arabia while more than a thousand miles away in Uganda the kind of Buganda is named *Kabaka.* Other kings are called *Kabazinga* and *Omukama.* On the eastern coast among the Swahili, the concept *Kali* denotes power while the same term refers to the black goddes *Kali* across the Indian Ocean among the negroes of India. *Kazi* is used among the Swahili to mean work or energy. Personal names all over East Africa manifest the current use of the term. There is for example *Kakuli* from the *Kamba* people and *Kamenju* from the *Kikuyus* in Kenya. *Kamaughisha* from the Bagishu and *Kasule* from the Baganda in Uganda. Opposite the Eastern Coast in Nigeria are cities like *Kano, Kaduna* and *Katsina* and the famous Emperor of Mali was *Kankan Musa* in

1326. The Ethiopian book of royal lineage is called **Kabra Naagst,** or imbued with serpent-power like the emblem on the pharoah's crown in Egypt. An ancient King of Ghana was called **Kannasai** and next to it is the modern country of **Kamaroon.** The president of Zambia is **Kaunda,** of Zanzibar as **Karume, Nkala** is a common name in Zimbabwe and Miriam Makeba says **Kauleza** when when she wants the listener to heed her son in South Africa. Thus throughout the length and breadth of Africa the term is used in relation to personal, community and group names and to describe concepts or to elaborate meaning. Whether Nilotic or Bantu, pastoral, agricultural or Riverine, rural or urban, all are unified by this ancient and deeply rooted connection. The Hausa peoples of West Africa use it with the exact purpose with which the term was invented in Egypt, addressing each other as **Kai!**, meaning your-self.

As we listen to these echos, and once we remember that the Sahara only began drying out around 1500 B.C., the pathways are open for the imagination to wander across the sand dunes, follow **Ka** across the desert and reconnect Egypt and its sisterly empires of Kush and Ethiopia to the mainstream of African culture.

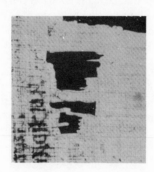

Behind Enemy Lines

Bernhard Mueller and Karel Dudesek

The guard at the military academy in Wroclaw clicked his heels. The two soldiers in olive-green uniforms and polished black boots saluted and entered the barracks square without any further controls. The name-tags on their jackets, McMueller and McDudesek, as well as the label US ARMY didn't cause any problems. We are in. American GIs inside Warsaw Pack barracks. Suddenly enemy imperialists are among the cadets. A former cadet has helped us to sneak in. Now we sit in the library surrounded by young soldiers in brown uniforms. We offer American cigarettes and answer all questions patiently. Why are we here? Haven't you heard about the new military treaties between the U.S., Yugoslavia, and Poland? We are from the US visitors army post in Cracow, we are on leave and in respect to our hosts we are not allowed to wear any uniform badges. Then we are left alone. In come 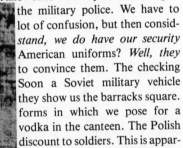 the military police. We have to show our Austrian passports. A lot of confusion, but then considerable relief. *You must understand, we do have our security regulations.* Why do we wear American uniforms? *Well, they are quite convenient.* That seems to convince them. The checking MP is wearing a uniform too. Soon a Soviet military vehicle with a driver is found. Proudly, they show us the barracks square. Then they lend us their dress uniforms in which we pose for a photo. That evening, we drink vodka in the canteen. The Polish railroad gives a more than 40% discount to soldiers. This is apparently valid for American GIs as well. The restaurant car is the ideal communication center. In the beginning nobody wants to take notice of the American soldiers, although we speak very openly in American slang. Then sudden astonishment, and again the usual questions and explanations. One of them wants a note from the GIs in his diary. *No more war — US Army.* Around midnight we are just waiting for the last connecting train — the dispatcher squeals on us. Again we are surrounded by military police. As we are finally finished with the control, the train is gone. In a Soviet jeep, they take us a couple of stations to catch up with the train. US soldiers jump off a Polish police car and run to catch a train. The conductor watching all this forgets to punch our tickets. We have no luck hitch-hiking to Wroclaw. The car drivers slow down when they see us but then they roar off. Finally a truckdriver gives us a ride but at the next stop he realizes that we wear US uniforms, and freaks out. In order to calm him down, we explain our true identity. Near Ribnik we have the opportunity to visit a mental hospital. Unchecked, we advance to the visitor's pavilion and immediately enter into a conversation with the inmates. They tell us about their wartime experiences and ask us for American cigarettes. Later some doctors come in, but they don't seem to notice us.

Next stop: Auschwitz. As a heavily frequented place of terror, the concentration camp is permanently under repair. Two workers install new ceramic insulators for the electric barbed wire. As soon as we want to take pictures, they disappear. So we take their tools and continue their work. In the movie theatre we see a documentary of American soldiers visiting the camp after the war. We also want to go into the archive (**For scholars and military personnel only**) and get a stack of brochures. In the restaurant, which looks like a student dining hall, the teacher of a class asks us mistrustfully whether we are real Americans. The young school girls admire us.

Later we go to the bus, and women and men with fur caps join us. *Russians,* the teacher informs us. When they see us in the dining hall they are evidently astonished. Later we sit in the express train to Warsaw. Polish soldiers offer us beer, but we decline. Our commander strictly forbade that. Our colleagues explain that they don't have to be that strict. Warsaw — main station. In the baggage checkroom, we meet some Vietnamese who kindly offer us cigarettes (American blend). They study medicine in Moscow.

The state studio-gallery is run by a young, dynamic art expert who is armed with the Art Diary 80. He thinks of himself as part of the cultural underground. Here in the *unwordly* art scene everything is in reverse. He was the only one who didn't want to believe that we are artists. Perhaps because we didn't appear in his Art Diary? As GIs we stop by the American embassy, of course. We apply for visas. The ambassador assures us: Being foreigners we will not be drafted. In the Austrian embassy they think that we, personally and diplomatically, are making fun of them when we ask them for an accompanying letter, which we could present on our walk through East Berlin in case of an arrest. The ambassador thinks we are draft resisters, in spite of the fact that McMueller and McDudesek are loyal members of the Federal Army. When we try to continue the discussion, they threaten us with Polish police, therefore we go to the GDR embassy without the accompanying letter. The GIs receive their transit visa for the trip to Berlin without hesitation. The secretary also informs us about an exhibition in the GDR institute of culture, photos of the GDR's People's Army.

In Gdansk we visit the headquarter of *Solidarnosc*. Before us, the new American ambassador was a guest at Walesa's, so now we ask for an appointment. The chief translator of Solidarnosc takes the initiative after we explained our project and the IUPA (Institute of Unknown Political Affairs). She thought it is all very funny. *Oh boy, we gonna have some fun with Walesa.* Walesa wants to know what we are doing and seems disconcerted. How can this be possible? Later, when we tell him about IPUA, we take off our uniform jackets — out of respect for *Unknown Political Affairs.* Photos with Walesa. We try to explain that with IUPA we seed direct contact with political personalities like him to convey our artistic actionistic sphere of life. Before we leave we give him a stick of sealing wax, to seal his treaties with the government.

On the train to East Berlin, no special controls. The Polish customs officers are interested in our Swiss pocket knives and want to buy them, but we explain that the knives are part of our equipment. We walk through checkpoint Charley, the only ones not searched. But in the KaDeWe Department store, we fall into an ambush. An American army patrol check us. We wear *field* dresses and not dress uniforms. A verbal running fight: *We are just coming from the East. Here everything is much worse. You cannot even move freely.* The MP doesn't understand anything. Our behavior seems to embarrass them. We use the moment of surprise and escape by escalator.

translation by Frank Mecklenburg

Fallen Angel

Sun Ra

I'm not a human. I never called anybody *mother.* The woman who's supposed to be my mother I call *other momma.* I never call nobody *mother.* I never call nobody *father.* I never felt that way. You have to realize this planet is not only inhabited by humans, it's inhabited by aliens too. They got the books say they fell from heaven with Satan. So, in mixed up among humans you have angels. The danger spot is the United States. You have more angels in the country than anywhere else. You see, it was planned.

I'll tell you something fantastic. It's unbelievable. They say that truth is stranger than fiction. Never in the history of the world has there been a case where you take a whole people and bring 'em into the country in the Commerce Department. Never before has that happened. It happened here. They bringing 'em in  through the Commerce Department. It was possible for aliens and angels and devils and demons to come in this country. They didn't need no passport. So then they'd come as displaced people. Perfect setup. So they come right on into the United States. They could come here and act like poor people, they could come here and act like slaves because they didn't keep up with what was happening. They just brought some people in...and said *Oh you they is nothing, they beastly.* They brought 'em in here and doin' that, they allowed anything to come in here.

If someone has the authority from the one who's causing the problem, it's no problem. It is not the nature of the human being to be self-destructive. So someone is causing it—there's a lot of confusion. But the Bible says God is the cause of confusion, that he confused the languages at the Tower of Babel. That's what it says. He did it, that's what they teach. So if he confuses, how do you do it? That's the point. If you find out how he did it, you can unravel the whole thing.

Well I found out how he did it. He did it with phonetics. Still telling the truth, but phonetics goes two ways. Like I just told you the words *virgin,* and *version,* it's like sun/son, *son* or *sun;* you got a lot of words spelled just alike, like *live* and *live,* and they go separate directions.

I don't really deal with life. I feel that life is death, you know. That it's a curse according to the Bible...Paul said, *Oh, who would deliver me from this body of death.* He said, *If a man is led to life he is led to death*...Another place in the Bible it says, *Their whole life through is nothing else but death.*

I understand English, you see, from a basic point of view, not from the American point of view, but from the Old English point of view which is very necessary if you get an old Bible. You start back there, this Bible translated by Englishmen, and you can find out they made a few mistakes. They made a few mistakes in the setters and the printers, too. And those are some problems you have in this country. Slight mistakes. Good ideas, but you can't even make the slight mistake 'cause everything will move that way.

In Egypt we played at the German Embassy over in Helipolis, which I didn't even know was the headquarters of the priests who dealt with Ra. I didn't know 'til I got to the United States and that that's where I had played. This big house. The Germans invited the Egyptians there and that's how the Egyptians knew I was in town 'cause they had never heard the band. So the cultural ministry wanted us to play so bad—*Our children need you and you have to go on TV! Don't ask us how much we're going to pay you. We pay our musicians so little; I can't even tell you what we will pay you, but it'll be after the program. That's the way we do things over here. Please play for our children.* The Egyptians don't seem to worry about time. They said we're gonna pick you up at three o'clock—send the bus out. Four o'clock—no bus; five o'clock—no bus; six o'clock I said, Well, we'll just get cabs and go down there. I called up and they said, *Well, the bus left at three o'clock.* So here we go down to the TV station and we set up maybe about six o'clock or six thirty and they said, *Well, you'll go on soon.* Seven o'clock came—the band is set up. Eight o'clock came—the band, nobody went to the washroom, nobody asked for no water. Nine o'clock came—we're still not on. Ten o'clock came. By eleven o'clock all at once, *Oh, we got to put the band on!* So we went on then. But now nobody went to the restroom. Nobody asked for no water and they saw some discipline. They can appreciate that. I'm going back to Egypt.

excerpted from an interview with Rick Theis

s e m i o t e x t (e)

BACK ISSUES

INDEX
Volume IV, 1981–84

FOUCAULT'S DILEMMA / *John Rajchman*
ON SOVIET FOREIGN POLICY / *Anders Stephanson*
MARXISM AND WORLD-HISTORICAL TRANSFORMATIONS / *James Petras*
IDEOLOGY AND THE METAPHYSICS OF CONTENT / *Michael E. Brown*
"WE MAKE WEEKENDS": LEISURE AND THE COMMODITY FORM / *Robert Goldman*
THE POLITICS OF YOUTH CULTURE: SOME OBSERVATIONS ON ROCK AND ROLL
IN AMERICAN CULTURE / *Lawrence Grossberg*
RECONSTRUCTING THE EXPERIMENT: POLITICS, IDEOLOGY, AND THE
AMERICAN NEW LEFT / *Stephen Eric Bronner*
OVERDETERMINATIONS: ON BLACK MARXISM IN BRITAIN / *Fredric Jameson*
THE APOCALYPSE OF ISLAM / *Norman O. Brown*

Social Text and the University of Minnesota Press (forthcoming)

Recently we have experienced a rather severe reaction against much of what the 60s is considered to have been. This collection of essays appraises the 60s from the point of view of the present, but in unapologetically sympathetic terms. The aim is certainly not to offer an uncritical defense of everything that happened during that period; it is rather to salvage what is interesting, useful, and politically important about it. The book thus makes no claim to give a complete history of the 60s. Rather, it presents a set of varied and straightforwardly partisan analyses and memories that, as a whole, constitutes the most serious overall assessment of the period yet to appear.

Stanley Aronowitz on the new left • Simon Frith on rock and roll • Cornel West on black politics
Ellen Willis on the origins of radical feminism • Fredric Jameson on 60s culture
Belden Fields on Maoism and Trotskyism in France • Colin Greer on the new ethnicity
Herman Rapaport on Vietnam

PLUS

Sohnya Sayres edits a special section of memoirs and statements including work by Paula Gunn Allen,
Martin Duberman, Alix Kates Shulman, Murray Bookchin, Joel Kovel, Paul Buhle, Charlie Shively,
Sol Yurick, and more!

PLUS

A lexicon of 60s language by Ralph Larkin and Daniel Foss
The book corresponds to Social Text #9-10 and will be available in May, 1984.

Subscriptions—Institution, $26.00; Regular, $14.00.
Order from SOCIAL TEXT, P.O. Box 450, 70 Greenwich Ave., New York, NY 10011.